CO

Po

Jenny Stacey

This is a Parragon Book
This edition published in 2000
Parragon
Queen Street House
4 Queen Street
Bath BA1 1HE, UK

Hardback ISBN: 0-75253-364-9
(Paperback ISBN: 0-75253-552-8)

Printed in China

Note

Cup measurements in this book are for American cups. Tablespoons are assumed to be 15 ml. Unless otherwise stated, milk is assumed to be full fat, eggs are medium and pepper is freshly ground black pepper.

Contents

Introduction

The potato is one of the world's most popular vegetables, cultivated in almost every country. There are many different varieties, native to these countries, each having a different quality or property. As a result of this, the potato suits most culinary styles and is perhaps the most versatile staple food available. It is recognised as one of the most important crops cultivated for human consumption, with Russia, Poland and Germany being the highest consumers, closely followed by Holland, Cyprus and Ireland.

On average we eat 109 kg/242 lb per head per annum, which is good news when you consider the nutritional properties of this best-loved tuber. The average 225 g/8 oz potato, containing 180 calories, has protein, starch for energy and fibre, as well as being a good source of vitamin C. Most of the vitamins are found just beneath the skin, which is why it is often suggested that potatoes are cooked in their skins and then peeled. If not cooked with fat, the potato has a great role to play in the slimming diet, a fact which has been disputed in the past.

However, the potato has not always been held in such high regard. It originated in South America and is thought to date back to as far as 3000 BC. First known as the papa and eaten by the Incas, the potato was unknown to the rest of the world until the sixteenth century when Spanish conquistador Francisco Pizarro captured Peru, which was famed for its richness in minerals. The mineral trade brought many people to Peru, who, in turn, carried the potato to the rest of the world. It was known by many names, which reflected the different cooking methods used by the Indians. Even this far back in its history, the potato was eaten fresh in season and dried by the Incas for use in the winter. Nowadays the storage life of potatoes and the different methods of preservation have increased its popularity in the food market.

The potato first arrived in Europe via Spain, and its name gradually changed from papa to battata. It became famous for both its nutritional and healing properties – the Italians believed it could heal a wound if the cooked flesh was rubbed into the infected area. One person in particular who believed this was Pope Pious IV, who was sent the potato when he was ill, and then grew his own crop in Italy. It then spread to Belgium, Germany, Switzerland and France, but did not reach the British Isles until Frances Drake stopped in the New World and shared his cargo (mainly potatoes) with the starving English colonists.

Later repatriated by Sir Walter Raleigh, the colonists brought the potato to Britain, where Raleigh grew the crop on his land. Raleigh was also responsible for taking the potato to Ireland, discovering that Irish soil was perfect for growing it. The starving Irish soon adopted the potato as their own and it became a mainstay of their diet.

Today there are many varieties of potato, each being suitable for different cooking methods, be it roasting, boiling, steaming, baking, mashing or frying. What makes it particularly versatile is the fact that it absorbs other flavours very readily and it has a consistency which lends itself to many uses.

CHOOSING AND USING POTATOES

Look for a firm, regular-shaped potato either red or yellow in colour with a smooth, tight skin. Avoid potatoes which are turning green or sprouting, as the flavour will be bitter and they will have higher levels of the natural toxicants called glycoalkaloids. Store potatoes in a cool, dark, dry place, as too much light turns them green.

The wide array of recipes that follow in this book will open up a world of delightful dishes, from hearty soups and salads, ideal light snacks and accompaniments to marvellous main meals and beautiful bakes, all made from that most reliable and delicious of staple foods, the potato. There is something for everyone – whether you are on a diet, a vegetarian or just a potato lover.

TYPES OF POTATO

There are about 3,000 known varieties of potato, but only about 100 of these are regularly grown. Of these, about 20 are found with ease on our greengrocers' and supermarket shelves. The following is a brief description of the most popular varieties and their uses, as a guide for the recipes in this book.

Charlotte New Potatoes

Craig Royal Red: *a main crop potato, ready in July, it is non-floury (mealy) and has a pink or red skin. A waxy potato, it is best for frying and boiling or using in salads.*

Cyprus New Potato: *found in late winter and spring, it is best simply scrubbed and boiled. Not a good mashing potato.*

Desiree: *a high quality, pink-skinned floury (mealy) potato, good for baking, frying, boiling and mashing.*

Home Guard: *generally the first of the new potatoes. It blackens easily and collapses on cooking, so it is best boiled lightly in its skin.*

Jersey Royal: *a delicious new potato. It appears from May to October, but is at its peak in August. It has a flaky skin and firm yellow flesh.*

King Edward: *a large potato which is creamy white, or sometimes yellow in colour. Ideal for all cooking methods, it is a very popular variety.*

Maris Piper: *a medium-firm potato with creamy white flesh. It is good for boiling and frying.*

New Potatoes: *these generally have a white flesh and grow quickly. They are dug up in early summer and are best scraped and boiled to use in salads or eaten with melted butter.*

Pentland Crown: *a thin-skinned, creamy white potato which is at its best in late winter. It has a floury (mealy) texture, making it ideal for mashing and baking.*

Pentland Hawk: *a firm, pale potato with pale yellow flesh, it is a general, all-purpose potato.*

Pentland Squire: *a firm, white-fleshed potato, which is suitable for all methods of cooking.*

Pink Fir Apple: *this long, knobbly potato has pink flesh and a firm, waxy texture. Good in salads.*

White Sweet Potato: *smaller than the yam, although interchangeable, it is yellow-fleshed with a drier texture. Best fried, boiled or casseroled, it is ideal with spices.*

Yam: *a red sweet potato which is orange-fleshed. It is best mashed in cakes and soufflés or roasted.*

Francine

Anya

Pentland Squire

Soups & Salads

Potatoes form the basis of many delicious and easy-to-prepare home-made soups, as they are the perfect thickening ingredient while adding a subtle flavour. With the addition of just a few ingredients, you have a whole selection of inexpensive soups at your fingertips. Add herbs, onion, garlic, meat, fish or vegetables, top with herbs or croûtons, simply serve with crusty bread for anything from a light starter to a filling meal.

Also featured in this chapter are salads based on potatoes. In addition to the creamy potato salads with herbs that are so popular, there are many other recipes to tempt your palate. There are well-known classics as well as innovative alternatives. There are salads suitable for light lunches as well as hearty main-course salads. Many are also ideal for barbecues (grills) and picnics.

Sweet Potato & Onion Soup

Serves 4

INGREDIENTS

2 tbsp vegetable oil
900 g/2 lb sweet potatoes, diced
1 carrot, diced
2 onions, sliced
2 garlic cloves, crushed
600 ml/1 pint/2½ cups vegetable stock
300 ml/½ pint/1¼ cups unsweetened orange juice
225 ml/8 fl oz/1 cup natural yogurt
2 tbsp chopped fresh coriander (cilantro)
salt and pepper

TO GARNISH:
coriander (cilantro) sprigs
orange rind

1 Heat the vegetable oil in a large saucepan and add the diced sweet potatoes and carrot, sliced onions and garlic. Sauté gently for 5 minutes, stirring constantly.

2 Pour in the vegetable stock and orange juice and bring them to the boil.

3 Reduce the heat to a simmer, cover the saucepan and cook the vegetables for 20 minutes or until the sweet potato and carrot cubes are tender.

4 Transfer the mixture to a food processor or blender in batches and process for 1 minute until puréed. Return the purée to the rinsed-out saucepan.

5 Stir in the natural yogurt and chopped coriander (cilantro) and season to taste. Serve the soup garnished with coriander (cilantro) sprigs and orange rind.

COOK'S TIP

This soup can be chilled before serving, if preferred. If chilling it, stir the yogurt into the dish just before serving. Serve in chilled bowls.

Potato, Apple & Rocket (Arugula) Soup

Serves 4

INGREDIENTS

4 tbsp butter
900 g/2 lb waxy potatoes, diced
1 red onion, quartered
1 tbsp lemon juice
1 litre/1$^{3}/_{4}$pints/4$^{1}/_{2}$ cups chicken stock
450 g/1 lb dessert apples, peeled and diced
pinch of ground allspice
50 g/1$^{3}/_{4}$ oz rocket (arugula) leaves
salt and pepper

TO GARNISH:
slices of red apple
chopped spring onions (scallions)

1 Melt the butter in a large saucepan and add the diced potatoes and sliced red onion. Sauté gently for 5 minutes, stirring constantly.

2 Add the lemon juice, chicken stock, diced apples and the ground allspice.

3 Bring to the boil, then reduce the heat to a simmer, cover the pan and cook for 15 minutes.

4 Add the rocket (arugula) to the soup and cook for a further 10 minutes until the potatoes are cooked through.

5 Transfer half of the soup to a food processor or blender and process for 1 minute. Return to the pan and stir the purée into the remaining soup.

6 Season to taste with salt and pepper. Ladle into hot soup bowls and garnish with the apple slices and chopped spring onions (scallions). Serve at once with warm crusty bread.

COOK'S TIP

If rocket (arugula) is unavailable, use baby spinach instead for a similar flavour.

Indian Potato & Pea Soup

Serves 4

INGREDIENTS

2 tbsp vegetable oil
225 g/8 oz floury (mealy) potatoes, diced
1 large onion, chopped
2 garlic cloves, crushed
1 tsp garam masala
1 tsp ground coriander
1 tsp ground cumin
900 ml/1½ pints/3¾cups vegetable stock
1 red chilli, chopped
100 g/3½ oz frozen peas
4 tbsp natural yogurt
salt and pepper
chopped fresh coriander (cilantro), to garnish

1 Heat the vegetable oil in a large saucepan and add the diced potatoes, onion and garlic. Sauté gently for about 5 minutes, stirring constantly.

2 Add the ground spices and cook for 1 minute, stirring all the time.

3 Stir in the vegetable stock and chopped red chilli and bring the mixture to the boil. Reduce the heat, cover the pan and simmer for 20 minutes until the potatoes begin to break down.

4 Add the peas and cook for a further 5 minutes. Stir in the yogurt and season to taste.

5 Pour into warmed soup bowls, garnish with chopped fresh coriander (cilantro) and serve hot with warm bread.

COOK'S TIP

Potatoes blend perfectly with spices, this soup being no exception. For an authentic Indian dish, serve this soup with warm naan bread.

VARIATION

For slightly less heat, deseed the chilli before adding it to the soup. Always wash your hands after handling chillies as they contain volatile oils that can irritate the skin and make your eyes burn if you touch your face.

Broccoli & Potato Soup

Serves 4

INGREDIENTS

2 tbsp olive oil
2 potatoes, diced
1 onion, diced
225 g/8 oz broccoli florets
125 g/4½ oz blue cheese, crumbled
1 litre/1¾ pints/4½ cups vegetable stock
150 ml/¼ pint/⅔ cup double (heavy) cream
pinch of paprika
salt and pepper

1 Heat the oil in a large saucepan and add the diced potatoes and onion. Sauté gently for 5 minutes, stirring constantly.

2 Reserve a few broccoli florets for the garnish and add the remaining broccoli to the pan. Add the cheese and stock.

3 Bring to the boil, then reduce the heat, cover the pan and simmer for 25 minutes until the potatoes are tender.

4 Transfer the soup to a food processor or blender in 2 batches and process until the mixture is a smooth purée.

5 Return the purée to a clean saucepan and stir in the cream and a pinch of paprika. Season to taste with salt and pepper.

6 Blanch the reserved broccoli florets in a little boiling water for about 2 minutes, then drain with a perforated spoon.

7 Pour the soup into warmed bowls and garnish with the broccoli florets and a sprinkling of paprika. Serve immediately.

COOK'S TIP

This soup freezes very successfully. Follow the method described here up to step 4, and freeze the soup after it has been puréed. Add the cream and paprika just before serving.

Potato & Dried Mushroom Soup

Serves 4

INGREDIENTS

2 tbsp vegetable oil
2 large floury (mealy) potatoes, sliced
1 onion, sliced
2 garlic cloves, crushed
1 litre/1¾ pints/4½ cups beef stock
25 g/1 oz dried mushrooms
2 celery sticks, sliced
2 tbsp brandy
salt and pepper

TOPPING:
3 tbsp butter
2 thick slices white bread, crusts removed
3 tbsp grated Parmesan cheese

TO GARNISH:
rehydrated dried mushrooms
parsley sprigs

1 Heat the vegetable oil in a large frying pan (skillet) and add the potato and onion slices and the garlic. Sauté gently for 5 minutes, stirring constantly.

2 Add the beef stock, dried mushrooms and the sliced celery. Bring to the boil, then reduce the heat to a simmer, cover the saucepan and cook the soup for 20 minutes until the potatoes are tender.

3 Meanwhile, melt the butter for the topping in the frying pan (skillet). Sprinkle the bread slices with the grated cheese and fry the slices in the butter for 1 minute on each side until crisp. Cut each slice into triangles.

4 Stir the brandy into the soup, season with salt and pepper. Pour into warmed bowls and top with the triangles. Serve garnished with mushrooms and parsley.

COOK'S TIP

Probably the most popular dried mushroom is the cep, but any variety will add a lovely flavour to this soup. If you do not wish to use dried mushrooms, add 125 g/4 oz sliced fresh mushrooms of your choice to the soup.

Potato, Split Pea & Cheese Soup

Serves 4

INGREDIENTS

2 tbsp vegetable oil
2 floury (mealy) potatoes, diced with skins left on
2 onions, diced
75 g/2¾ oz split green peas
1 litre/1¾ pints/4½ cups vegetable stock
5 tbsp grated Gruyère cheese
salt and pepper

CROUTONS:
3 tbsp butter
1 garlic clove, crushed
1 tbsp chopped fresh parsley
1 thick slice white bread, cubed

1 Heat the vegetable oil in a large saucepan and add the diced potatoes and onions. Sauté gently for about 5 minutes, stirring constantly.

2 Add the split green peas to the pan and stir to mix together well.

3 Pour the vegetable stock into the pan and bring to the boil. Reduce the heat to a simmer and cook for 35 minutes until the potatoes are tender and the split peas cooked.

4 Meanwhile, make the croutons. Melt the butter in a frying pan (skillet). Add the garlic, chopped parsley and bread cubes and cook for about 2 minutes, turning frequently until the bread cubes are golden brown on all sides.

5 Stir the grated cheese into the soup and season to taste with salt and pepper.

6 Pour the soup into warmed bowls and sprinkle the croutons on top. Serve at once.

VARIATION

Red lentils could be used instead of split green peas if preferred, for a richly coloured soup. Add a large pinch of brown sugar to the recipe for sweetness if red lentils are used.

2

4

5

Leek, Potato & Bacon Soup

Serves 4

INGREDIENTS

25 g/1 oz/2 tbsp butter
175 g/6 oz potatoes, diced
4 leeks, shredded
2 garlic cloves, crushed
100 g/3½ oz smoked bacon, diced
900 ml/1½ pints/3¾ cups vegetable stock
225 ml/8 fl oz/1 cup double (heavy) cream
2 tbsp chopped fresh parsley
salt and pepper

TO GARNISH:
vegetable oil
1 leek, shredded

1 Melt the butter in a large saucepan and add the diced potatoes, shredded leeks, garlic and diced bacon. Sauté gently for 5 minutes, stirring constantly.

2 Add the vegetable stock and bring to the boil. Reduce the heat, cover the saucepan and simmer for 20 minutes until the potatoes are cooked. Stir in the double (heavy) cream.

3 Meanwhile, make the garnish. Half-fill a pan with oil and heat to 180°C–190°C/350°F–375°F or until a cube of bread browns in 30 seconds. Add the shredded leek and deep-fry for 1 minute until browned and crisp, taking care as the leek contains water. Drain the leek thoroughly on paper towels and reserve.

4 Reserve a few pieces of potato, leek and bacon and set aside. Put the rest of the soup in a food processor or blender in batches and process each batch for 30 seconds. Return the puréed soup to a clean saucepan and heat through.

5 Stir in the reserved vegetables, bacon and parsley and season to taste. Pour into warmed bowls and garnish with the fried leeks.

VARIATION

For a lighter soup, omit the cream and stir yogurt or crème fraîche into the soup at the end of the cooking time.

Potato, Cabbage & Chorizo Soup

Serves 4

INGREDIENTS

2 tbsp olive oil
3 large potatoes, cubed
2 red onions, quartered
1 garlic clove, crushed
1 litre/1¾ pints/4½ cups pork or vegetable stock
150 g/5½ oz Savoy cabbage, shredded
50 g/1¾ oz chorizo sausage, sliced
salt and pepper
paprika, to garnish

1 Heat the olive oil in a large saucepan and add the cubed potatoes, quartered red onions and garlic. Sauté gently for 5 minutes, stirring constantly.

2 Add the pork or vegetable stock and bring to the boil. Reduce the heat and cover the saucepan. Simmer the vegetables for about 20 minutes until the potatoes are tender.

3 Process the soup in a food processor or blender in 2 batches for 1 minute each. Return the puréed soup to a clean pan.

4 Add the shredded Savoy cabbage and sliced chorizo sausage to the pan and cook for a further 7 minutes. Season to taste.

5 Ladle the soup into warmed soup bowls, garnish with a sprinkling of paprika and serve.

VARIATION

If chorizo sausage is not available, you could use any other spicy sausage or even salami in its place.

COOK'S TIP

Chorizo sausage requires no pre-cooking. In this recipe, it is added towards the end of the cooking time so that it does not overpower the other flavours in the soup.

Chinese Potato & Pork Broth

Serves 4

INGREDIENTS

1 litre/1¾ pints/4½ cups chicken stock
2 large potatoes, diced
2 tbsp rice wine vinegar
125 g/4½ oz pork fillet, sliced
2 tbsp cornflour (cornstarch)
4 tbsp water
1 tbsp light soy sauce
1 tsp sesame oil
1 carrot, cut into very thin strips
1 tsp ginger root, chopped
3 spring onions (scallions), sliced thinly
1 red (bell) pepper, sliced
225 g/8 oz can bamboo shoots, drained

1 Add the chicken stock, diced potatoes and 1 tbsp of the rice wine vinegar to a saucepan and bring to the boil. Reduce the heat until the stock is just simmering.

2 In a small bowl, mix the cornflour (cornstarch) with the water. Stir the mixture into the hot stock.

3 Bring the stock back to the boil, stirring until thickened, then reduce the heat until it is just simmering again.

4 Place the pork slices in a shallow dish and season with the remaining rice wine vinegar, soy sauce and sesame oil.

5 Add the pork slices, carrot strips and chopped ginger to the stock and cook for 10 minutes. Stir in the sliced spring onions (scallions), red (bell) pepper and bamboo shoots. Cook for a further 5 minutes.

6 Pour the soup into warmed bowls and serve immediately.

COOK'S TIP

Sesame oil is very strongly flavoured and is, therefore, only used in small quantities.

VARIATION

For extra heat, add 1 chopped red chilli or 1 tsp of chilli powder to the soup in step 5.

Chunky Potato & Beef Soup

Serves 4

INGREDIENTS

2 tbsp vegetable oil
225 g/8 oz braising or frying steak, cut into strips
225 g/8 oz new potatoes, halved
1 carrot, diced
2 celery sticks, sliced
2 leeks, sliced
900 ml/1½ pints/3¾ cups beef stock
8 baby sweetcorn cobs, sliced
1 bouquet garni
2 tbsp dry sherry
salt and pepper
chopped fresh parsley, to garnish

1 Heat the vegetable oil in a large saucepan. Add the strips of meat and cook for 3 minutes, turning constantly.

2 Add the halved potatoes, diced carrot and sliced celery and leeks. Cook for a further 5 minutes, stirring.

3 Pour the beef stock into the saucepan and bring to the boil. Reduce the heat until the liquid is simmering, then add the sliced baby sweetcorn cobs and the bouquet garni.

4 Cook the soup for a further 20 minutes or until the meat and all of the vegetables are cooked through.

5 Remove the bouquet garni from the saucepan and discard. Stir the dry sherry into the soup and then season to taste with salt and pepper.

6 Pour the soup into warmed bowls and garnish with the chopped fresh parsley. Serve at once, accompanied by chunks of fresh crusty bread.

COOK'S TIP

Make double the quantity of soup and freeze the remainder in a rigid container for later use. When ready to use, leave in the refrigerator to defrost thoroughly, then heat until piping hot.

Potato & Mixed Fish Soup

Serves 4

INGREDIENTS

2 tbsp vegetable oil
450 g/1 lb small new potatoes, halved
1 bunch spring onions (scallions), sliced
1 yellow (bell) pepper, sliced
2 garlic cloves, crushed
225 ml/8 fl oz/1 cup dry white wine
600 ml/1 pint/2½ cups fish stock
225 g/8 oz white fish fillet, skinned and cubed
225 g/8 oz smoked cod fillet, skinned and cubed
2 tomatoes, peeled, seeded and chopped
100 g/3½ oz peeled cooked prawns (shrimp)
150 ml/¼ pint/⅔ cup double (heavy) cream
2 tbsp shredded fresh basil

1 Heat the vegetable oil in a large saucepan and add the halved potatoes, sliced spring onions (scallions) and (bell) pepper and the garlic. Sauté gently for 3 minutes, stirring constantly.

2 Add the white wine and fish stock and bring to the boil. Reduce the heat and simmer for 10–15 minutes.

3 Add the cubed fish fillets and the tomatoes to the soup and continue to cook for 10 minutes or until the fish is cooked through.

4 Stir in the prawns (shrimp), cream and shredded basil and cook for 2–3 minutes. Pour the soup into warmed bowls and serve.

COOK'S TIP

The basil is added at the end of the cooking time as the flavour is destroyed by heat.

VARIATION

For a soup which is slightly less rich, omit the wine and stir natural yogurt into the soup instead of the double (heavy) cream.

Potato, Mixed Bean & Apple Salad

Serves 4

INGREDIENTS

225 g/8 oz new potatoes, scrubbed and quartered
225 g/8 oz mixed canned beans, such as red kidney beans, flageolet and borlotti beans, drained and rinsed
1 red dessert apple, diced and tossed in 1 tbsp lemon juice
1 small yellow (bell) pepper, diced
1 shallot, sliced
½ head fennel, sliced
oak leaf lettuce leaves

DRESSING:
1 tbsp red wine vinegar
2 tbsp olive oil
½ tbsp American mustard
1 garlic clove, crushed
2 tsp chopped fresh thyme

1 Cook the quartered potatoes in a saucepan of boiling water for 15 minutes until tender. Drain and transfer to a mixing bowl.

2 Add the mixed beans to the potatoes with the diced apple and yellow (bell) pepper, and the sliced shallots and fennel. Mix well, taking care not to break up the cooked potatoes.

3 In a bowl, whisk all the dressing ingredients together, then pour it over the potato salad.

4 Line a plate or salad bowl with the oak leaf and spoon the potato mixture into the centre. Serve immediately.

VARIATION

Use Dijon or wholegrain mustard in place of American mustard for a different flavour.

COOK'S TIP

Canned beans are used here for convenience, but dried beans may be used instead. Soak for 8 hours or overnight, drain and place in a saucepan. Cover with water, bring to the boil and boil for 10 minutes, then simmer until tender.

2

3

4

Potato, Beetroot & Cucumber Salad with Dill Dressing

Serves 4

INGREDIENTS

450 g/1 lb waxy potatoes, diced
4 small cooked beetroot, sliced
½ small cucumber, sliced thinly
2 large dill pickles, sliced
1 red onion, halved and sliced
dill sprigs, to garnish

DRESSING:
1 garlic clove, crushed
2 tbsp olive oil
2 tbsp red wine vinegar
2 tbsp chopped fresh dill
salt and pepper

1 Cook the diced potatoes in a saucepan of boiling water for 15 minutes or until tender. Drain and leave to cool.

2 When cool, mix the potato and beetroot together in a bowl and set aside.

3 Line a salad platter with the slices of cucumber, dill pickles and red onion. Spoon the potato and beetroot mixture into the centre of the platter.

4 In a small bowl, whisk all the dressing ingredients together, then pour it over the salad.

5 Serve the salad immediately, garnished with dill sprigs.

COOK'S TIP

If making the salad in advance, do not mix the beetroot and potatoes until just before serving, as the beetroot will bleed its colour.

VARIATION

Line the salad platter with 2 heads of chicory (endive), separated into leaves, and arrange the cucumber, dill pickle and red onion slices on top of the leaves.

2

3

4

Potato, Radish & Cucumber Salad

Serves 4

INGREDIENTS

450 g/1 lb new potatoes, scrubbed and halved
½ cucumber, sliced thinly
2 tsp salt
1 bunch radishes, sliced thinly

DRESSING:
1 tbsp Dijon mustard
2 tbsp olive oil
1 tbsp white wine vinegar
2 tbsp mixed chopped herbs

1 Cook the potatoes in a saucepan of boiling water for 10-15 minutes or until tender. Drain and leave to cool.

2 Meanwhile spread out the cucumber slices on a plate and sprinkle with the salt. Leave to stand for 30 minutes, then rinse under cold running water and pat dry with paper towels.

3 Arrange the cucumber and radish slices on a serving plate in a decorative pattern and pile the cooked potatoes in the centre of the slices.

4 In a small bowl, mix the dressing ingredients together. Pour the dressing over the salad, tossing well to coat all of the salad ingredients. Leave to chill in the refrigerator before serving.

VARIATION

Dijon mustard has a mild clean taste which is perfect for this salad as it does not overpower the other flavours. If unavailable, use another mild mustard – English mustard is too strong for this salad.

COOK'S TIP

The cucumber adds not only colour but a real freshness to the salad. It is salted and left to stand to remove the excess water which would make the salad soggy. Wash the cucumber well to remove all of the salt, before adding to the salad.

2

2

3

Sweet Potato & Banana Salad

Serves 4

INGREDIENTS

450 g/1 lb sweet potatoes, diced
50 g/1¾ oz/10 tsp butter
1 tbsp lemon juice
1 garlic clove, crushed
1 red (bell) pepper, diced
1 green (bell) pepper, diced
2 bananas, sliced thickly
2 thick slices white bread, crusts removed, diced
salt and pepper

DRESSING:
2 tbsp clear honey
2 tbsp chopped fresh chives
2 tbsp lemon juice
2 tbsp olive oil

1 Cook the sweet potatoes in a saucepan of boiling water for 10–15 minutes until tender. Drain thoroughly and reserve.

2 Meanwhile, melt the butter in a frying pan (skillet). Add the lemon juice, garlic and (bell) peppers and cook for 3 minutes, turning constantly.

3 Add the banana slices to the pan and cook for 1 minute. Remove the bananas from the pan with a slotted spoon and stir into the potatoes.

4 Add the bread cubes to the frying pan (skillet) and cook for 2 minutes, turning frequently until they are golden brown on all sides.

5 Mix the dressing ingredients together in a small saucepan and heat until the honey is runny.

6 Spoon the potato mixture into a serving dish and season to taste with salt and pepper. Pour the dressing over the potatoes and sprinkle the croûtons over the top. Serve immediately.

COOK'S TIP

Use firm, slightly underripe bananas in this recipe as they won't turn soft and mushy when fried.

Sweet Potato & Nut Salad

Serves 4

INGREDIENTS

450 g/1 lb sweet potatoes, diced
2 celery sticks, sliced
125 g/4½ oz celeriac, grated
2 spring onions (scallions), sliced
50 g/1¾ oz pecan nuts, chopped
2 heads chicory (endive), separated
1 tsp lemon juice
thyme sprigs, to garnish

DRESSING:
4 tbsp vegetable oil
1 tbsp garlic wine vinegar
1 tsp soft light brown sugar
2 tsp chopped fresh thyme

1 Cook the sweet potatoes in a saucepan of boiling water for 5 minutes until tender. Drain thoroughly and leave to cool.

2 When cooled, stir in the celery, celeriac, spring onions (scallions) and pecan nuts.

3 Line a salad plate with the chicory (endive) leaves and sprinkle with lemon juice.

4 Spoon the potato mixture into the centre of the leaves.

5 In a small bowl, whisk the dressing ingredients together.

6 Pour the dressing over the salad and serve at once, garnished with thyme sprigs.

VARIATION

For variety, replace the garlic wine vinegar in the dressing with a different flavoured oil, such as chilli or herb.

COOK'S TIP

Sweet potatoes do not store as well as ordinary potatoes. It is best to store them in a cool, dark place (not the refrigerator) and use within 1 week of purchase.

2

3

6

Indian Potato Salad

Serves 4

INGREDIENTS

4 medium floury (mealy) potatoes, diced
75 g/2¾ oz small broccoli florets
1 small mango, diced
4 spring onions (scallions), sliced
salt and pepper
small cooked spiced poppadoms, to serve

DRESSING:
½ tsp ground cumin
½ tsp ground coriander
1 tbsp mango chutney
150 ml/¼ pint/⅔ cup natural yogurt
1 tsp ginger root, chopped
2 tbsp chopped fresh coriander (cilantro)

1 Cook the potatoes in a saucepan of boiling water for 10 minutes or until tender. Drain and place in a mixing bowl.

2 Meanwhile, blanch the broccoli florets in a separate saucepan of boiling water for 2 minutes. Drain well and add to the potatoes in the bowl.

3 When the potatoes and broccoli have cooled, add the diced mango and sliced spring onions (scallions). Season to taste with salt and pepper and mix well to combine.

4 In a small bowl, stir all of the dressing ingredients together.

5 Spoon the dressing over the potato mixture and mix together carefully, taking care not to break up the potatoes and broccoli.

6 Serve the salad at once, accompanied by small cooked spiced poppadoms.

COOK'S TIP

Mix the dressing ingredients together in advance and leave to chill in the refrigerator for a few hours in order for a stronger flavour to develop.

Mexican Potato Salad

Serves 4

INGREDIENTS

4 large waxy potatoes, sliced
1 ripe avocado
1 tsp olive oil
1 tsp lemon juice
1 garlic clove, crushed
1 onion, chopped
2 large tomatoes, sliced
1 green chilli, chopped
1 yellow (bell) pepper, sliced
2 tbsp chopped fresh coriander
salt and pepper
lemon wedges, to garnish

1 Cook the potato slices in a saucepan of boiling water for 10–15 minutes or until tender. Drain and leave to cool.

2 Meanwhile, cut the avocado in half and remove the stone. Using a spoon, scoop the avocado flesh from the 2 halves and place in a mixing bowl.

3 Mash the avocado flesh with a fork and stir in the olive oil, lemon juice, garlic and chopped onion. Cover the bowl with cling film (plastic wrap) and set aside.

4 Mix the tomatoes, chilli and yellow (bell) pepper together and transfer to a salad bowl with the potato slices.

5 Spoon the avocado mixture on top and sprinkle with the coriander (cilantro). Season to taste and serve garnished with lemon wedges.

COOK'S TIP

Mixing the avocado flesh with lemon juice prevents it from turning brown once exposed to the air.

VARIATION

Omit the green chilli from this salad if you do not like hot dishes.

3

4

5

Potato Nests of Chinese Salad

Serves 4

INGREDIENTS

POTATO NESTS:
450 g/1 lb floury (mealy) potatoes, grated
125 g/4½ oz/1 cup cornflour (cornstarch)
vegetable oil, for frying
fresh chives, to garnish

SALAD:
125 g/4½ oz pineapple, cubed
1 green (bell) pepper, cut into strips
1 carrot, cut into thin strips
50 g/1¾ oz mangetout (snowpeas), sliced thickly
4 baby sweetcorn cobs, halved lengthways
25 g/1 oz beansprouts
2 spring onions (scallions), sliced

DRESSING:
1 tbsp clear honey
1 tsp light soy sauce
1 garlic clove, crushed
1 tsp lemon juice

1 To make the nests, rinse the potatoes several times in cold water. Drain well on paper towels and place them in a mixing bowl. Add the cornflour (cornstarch), mixing well to coat the potatoes.

2 Half fill a wok with vegetable oil and heat until smoking. Line a 15 cm/6 inch diameter wire sieve with a quarter of the potato mixture and press another sieve of the same size on top.

3 Lower the sieves into the oil and cook for 2 minutes until the potato nest is golden brown and crisp. Remove from the wok, allowing the excess oil to drain off.

4 Repeat 3 more times to use up all of the mixture and make a total of 4 nests. Leave to cool.

5 Mix the salad ingredients together in a bowl, then spoon into the potato baskets.

6 Mix the dressing ingredients together in a bowl. Pour the dressing over the salad, garnish with chives and serve immediately.

COOK'S TIP

For this recipe, the potatoes must be washed well before use to remove excess starch. Make sure the potatoes are completely dry before cooking in the fat to prevent spitting.

1

2

3

Potato, Rocket (Arugula) & Apple Salad

Serves 4

INGREDIENTS

2 large potatoes, unpeeled and sliced
2 green dessert apples, diced
1 tsp lemon juice
25 g/1 oz walnut pieces
125 g/4½ oz goat's cheese, cubed
150 g/5½ oz rocket (arugula) leaves
salt and pepper

DRESSING:
2 tbsp olive oil
1 tbsp red wine vinegar
1 tsp clear honey
1 tsp fennel seeds

1 Cook the potatoes in a pan of boiling water for 15 minutes until tender. Drain and leave to cool. Transfer the cooled potatoes to a serving bowl.

2 Toss the diced apples in the lemon juice, drain and stir into the cold potatoes.

3 Add the walnut pieces, cheese cubes and rocket (arugula) leaves, then toss the salad to mix.

4 In a small bowl, whisk the dressing ingredients together and pour the dressing over the salad. Serve immediately.

VARIATION

Use smoked or blue cheese instead of goat's cheese, if you prefer. In addition, if rocket (arugula) is unavailable use baby spinach instead.

COOK'S TIP

Serve this salad immediately to prevent the apple from discolouring. Alternatively, prepare all of the other ingredients in advance and add the apple at the last minute.

Potato & Mixed Vegetable Salad with Lemon Mayonnaise

Serves 4

INGREDIENTS

450 g/1 lb waxy new potatoes, scrubbed
1 carrot, cut into matchsticks
225 g/8 oz cauliflower florets
225 g/8 oz baby sweetcorn cobs, halved lenghtways
175 g/6 oz French (green) beans
175 g/6 oz ham, diced
50 g/1$^{3}/_{4}$ oz mushrooms, sliced
salt and pepper

DRESSING:
2 tbsp chopped fresh parsley
150 ml/$^{1}/_{4}$ pint/$^{2}/_{3}$ cup mayonnaise
150 ml/$^{1}/_{4}$ pint/$^{2}/_{3}$ cup natural yogurt
4 tsp lemon juice
rind of 1 lemon
2 tsp fennel seeds

1 Cook the potatoes in a pan of boiling water for 15 minutes or until tender. Drain and leave to cool. When the potatoes are cold, slice them thinly.

2 Meanwhile, cook the carrot matchsticks, cauliflower florets, baby sweetcorn cobs and French (green) beans in a pan of boiling water for 5 minutes. Drain well and leave to cool.

3 Reserve 1 tsp of the chopped parsley for the garnish. In a bowl, mix the remaining dressing ingredients together.

4 Arrange the vegetables on a salad platter and top with the ham strips and sliced mushrooms.

5 Spoon the dressing over the the salad and garnish with the reserved parsley. Serve at once.

COOK'S TIP

For a really quick salad, use a frozen packet of mixed vegetables, thawed, instead of fresh vegetables.

1

2

4

Indonesian Potato & Chicken Salad

Serves 4

INGREDIENTS

- 4 large waxy potatoes, diced
- 300 g/10½ oz fresh pineapple, diced
- 2 carrots, grated
- 175 g/6 oz beansprouts
- 1 bunch spring onions (scallions), sliced
- 1 large courgette (zucchini), cut into matchsticks
- 3 celery sticks, cut into matchsticks
- 175 g/6 oz unsalted peanuts
- 2 cooked chicken breast fillets, about 125 g/4½ oz each, sliced

DRESSING:

- 6 tbsp crunchy peanut butter
- 6 tbsp olive oil
- 2 tbsp light soy sauce
- 1 red chilli, chopped
- 2 tsp sesame oil
- 4 tsp lime juice

1 Cook the diced potatoes in a saucepan of boiling water for 10 minutes or until tender. Drain and leave to cool.

2 Transfer the cooled potatoes to a salad bowl.

3 Add the pineapple, carrots, beansprouts, spring onions (scallions), courgette (zucchini), celery, peanuts and sliced chicken to the potatoes. Toss well to mix all the salad ingredients together.

4 To make the dressing, put the peanut butter in a small bowl and gradually whisk in the olive oil and light soy sauce.

5 Stir in the chopped red chilli, sesame oil and lime juice. Mix until well combined.

6 Pour the spicy dressing over the salad and toss lightly to coat all of the ingredients. Serve the salad immediately, garnished with the lime wedges.

COOK'S TIP

Unsweetened canned pineapple may be used in place of the fresh pineapple for convenience. If only sweetened canned pineapple is available, drain it and rinse under cold running water before using.

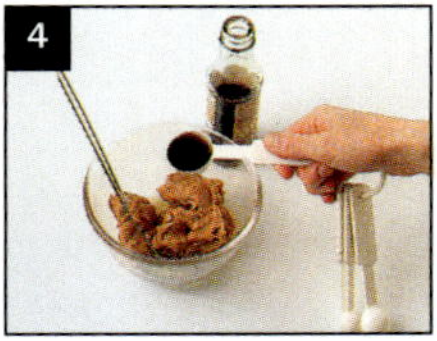

Potato & Spicy Chicken Salad

Serves 4

INGREDIENTS

2 skinned chicken breast fillets, about 125 g/4½ oz each
25 g/1 oz/2 tbsp butter
1 red chilli, chopped
1 tbsp clear honey
½ tsp ground cumin
2 tbsp chopped fresh coriander (cilantro)
2 large potatoes, diced
50 g/1¾ oz thin green beans, halved
1 red (bell) pepper, cut into thin strips
2 tomatoes, seeded and diced

DRESSING:
2 tbsp olive oil
pinch of chilli powder
1 tbsp garlic wine vinegar
pinch of caster sugar
1 tbsp chopped fresh coriander (cilantro)

1 Cut the chicken into thin strips. Melt the butter in a pan over a medium heat and add the chicken, chilli, honey and cumin. Cook for 10 minutes, turning until cooked through.

2 Transfer the mixture to a bowl, leave to cool, then stir in the coriander (cilantro).

3 Meanwhile, cook the diced potatoes in a saucepan of boiling water for 10 minutes until tender. Drain and leave to cool.

4 Blanch the green beans in boiling water for 3 minutes, drain and leave to cool. Mix the green beans and potatoes together in a salad bowl.

5 Add the (bell) pepper strips and diced tomatoes to the potatoes and beans. Stir in the spicy chicken mixture.

6 In a small bowl, whisk the dressing ingredients together and pour the dressing over the salad, tossing well. Serve at once.

VARIATION

If you prefer, use lean turkey meat instead of the chicken for a slightly stronger flavour. Use the white meat for the best appearance and flavour.

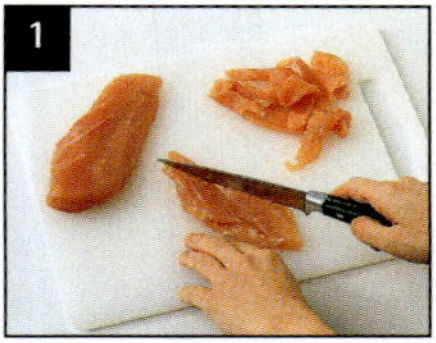
1

4

5

Grilled (Broiled) New Potato Salad

Serves 4

INGREDIENTS

650 g/1½ lb new potatoes, scrubbed
3 tbsp olive oil
2 tbsp chopped fresh thyme
1 tsp paprika
4 rashers smoked bacon
salt and pepper
parsley sprig, to garnish

DRESSING:
4 tbsp mayonnaise
1 tbsp garlic wine vinegar
2 garlic cloves, crushed
1 tbsp chopped fresh parsley

1 Cook the new potatoes in a saucepan of boiling water for 10 minutes. Drain thoroughly.

2 Mix the olive oil, chopped thyme and paprika together and pour the mixture over the warm potatoes.

3 Place the bacon rashers under a preheated medium grill (broiler) and cook for 5 minutes, turning once until crisp. When cooked, roughly chop the bacon and keep warm.

4 Transfer the potatoes to the grill (broiler) pan and cook for 10 minutes, turning once.

5 Mix the dressing ingredients in a small serving bowl. Transfer the potatoes and bacon to a large serving bowl. Season with salt and pepper and mix together.

6 Spoon over the dressing, garnish with a parsley sprig and serve immediately for a warm salad. Alternatively, leave to cool and serve chilled.

VARIATION

Add spicy sausage to the salad in place of bacon – you do not need to cook it under the grill (broiler) before adding to the salad.

2

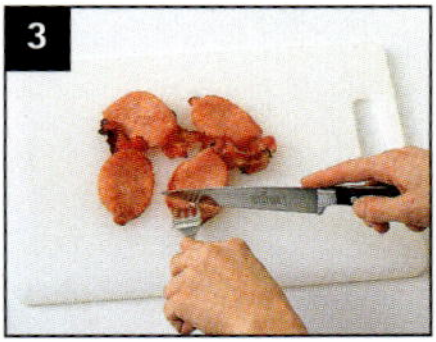
3

4

Potato & Italian Sausage Salad

Serves 4

INGREDIENTS

450 g/1 lb waxy potatoes
1 raddichio or lollo rosso lettuce
1 green (bell) pepper, sliced
175 g/6 oz Italian sausage, sliced
1 red onion, halved and sliced
125 g/4½ oz sun-dried tomatoes, sliced
2 tbsp shredded fresh basil

DRESSING:
1 tbsp balsamic vinegar
1 tsp tomato purée (paste)
2 tbsp olive oil
salt and pepper

1 Cook the potatoes in a saucepan of boiling water for 20 minutes or until cooked through. Drain and leave to cool.

2 Line a large serving platter with the radicchio or lollo rosso lettuce leaves.

3 Slice the cooled potatoes and arrange them in layers on the lettuce-lined serving platter together with the sliced green (bell) pepper, sliced Italian sausage, red onion, sun-dried tomatoes and shredded fresh basil.

4 In a small bowl, whisk the balsamic vinegar, tomato purée (paste) and olive oil together and season to taste with salt and pepper. Pour the dressing over the potato salad and serve immediately.

COOK'S TIP

You can use either packets of sun-dried tomatoes or jars of sun-dried tomatoes in oil. If using tomatoes packed in oil, simply rinse the oil from the tomatoes and pat them dry on paper towels before using.

VARIATION

Any sliced Italian sausage or salami can be used in this salad. Italy is home of the salami and there are numerous varieties to choose from – those from the south tend to be more highly spiced than those from the north of the country.

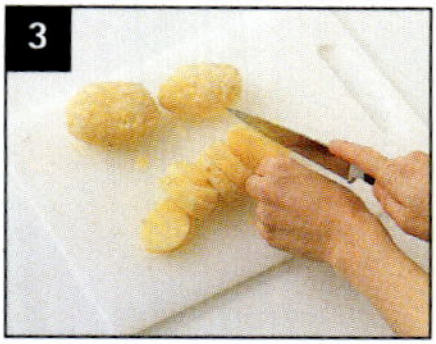

Potato & Lobster Salad with Lime Dressing

Serves 4

INGREDIENTS

450 g/1 lb waxy potatoes, scrubbed and sliced
225 g/8 oz cooked lobster meat
150 ml/¼ pint/⅔ cup mayonnaise
2 tbsp lime juice
finely grated rind of 1 lime
1 tbsp chopped fresh parsley
2 tbsp olive oil
2 tomatoes, seeded and diced
2 hard-boiled (hard-cooked) eggs, quartered
1 tbsp quartered stoned (pitted) green olives
salt and pepper

1 Cook the potatoes in a saucepan of boiling water for 10-15 minutes or until cooked through. Drain and reserve.

2 Remove the lobster meat from the shell and separate it into large pieces.

3 In a bowl, mix together the mayonnaise, 1 tbsp of the lime juice, half the grated lime rind and half the chopped parsley, then set aside.

4 In a separate bowl, whisk the remaining lime juice with the olive oil and pour the dressing over the potatoes. Arrange the potatoes on a serving plate.

5 Top with the lobster meat, tomatoes, eggs and olives. Season with salt and pepper and sprinkle with the reserved parsley.

6 Spoon the mayonnaise on to the centre of the salad, top with the reserved rind and serve.

COOK'S TIP

As shellfish is used in this salad, serve it immediately, or keep covered and chilled for up to 1 hour before serving.

VARIATION

Crabmeat or prawns (shrimp) may be used instead of the lobster, if you prefer.

Potato & Tuna Salad

Serves 4

INGREDIENTS

450 g/1 lb new potatoes, scrubbed and quartered
1 green (bell) pepper, sliced
50 g/1¾ oz canned sweetcorn, drained
1 red onion, sliced
300 g/10½ oz canned tuna in brine, drained and flaked
2 tbsp chopped stoned (pitted) black olives
salt and pepper
lime wedges, to garnish

DRESSING:
2 tbsp mayonnaise
2 tbsp soured cream
1 tbsp lime juice
2 garlic cloves, crushed
finely grated rind of 1 lime

1 Cook the potatoes in a saucepan of boiling water for 15 minutes until tender. Drain and leave to cool in a mixing bowl.

2 Gently stir in the sliced green (bell) pepper, sweetcorn and sliced red onion.

3 Spoon the potato mixture into a large serving bowl and arrange the flaked tuna and chopped black olives over the top. Season the salad generously with salt and pepper.

4 To make the dressing, mix together the mayonnaise, soured cream, lime juice, garlic and lime rind in a bowl.

5 Spoon the dressing over the tuna and olives, garnish with lime wedges and serve.

COOK'S TIP

Served with a crisp white wine, this salad makes the perfect light lunch for summer or winter.

VARIATION

Green beans and hard-boiled (hard-cooked) egg slices can be added to the salad for a more traditional Salade Niçoise.

Snacks & Light Meals

Potatoes are so versatile that they can be used as a base to create a whole array of tempting light meals and satisfying snacks. They are also extremely nutritious, as the carbohydrate they contain will give a welcome energy boost. As potatoes have a fairly neutral flavour, they can be teamed with a variety of other ingredients and flavours to make lots of interesting meals and snacks.

This chapter contains a range of tempting snacks, including Paprika Potato Crisps, Spicy Potato-filled Naan Breads and Spanish Tortilla, which are quick and easy to make and will satisfy those mid-morning or mid-afternoon hunger pangs! They also come in handy if an expected visitor drops by.

This chapter also contains a range of delicious yet light meals which are ideal if you feel slightly peckish rather than ravenously hungry – try Potato Omelette with Feta Cheese & Spinach or Potato Pancakes with Soured Cream & Salmon.

Potato & Bean Pâté

Serves 4

INGREDIENTS

100 g/3½ oz floury (mealy) potatoes, diced
225 g/8 oz mixed canned beans, such as borlotti, flageolet and kidney beans, drained
1 garlic clove, crushed
2 tsp lime juice
1 tbsp chopped fresh coriander (cilantro)
2 tbsp natural yogurt
salt and pepper
chopped fresh coriander (cilantro), to garnish

1 Cook the potatoes in a saucepan of boiling water for 10 minutes until tender. Drain well and mash.

2 Transfer the potato to a food processor or blender and add the beans, garlic, lime juice and the fresh coriander (cilantro). Season the mixture and process for 1 minute to make a smooth purée. Alternatively, mix the beans with the potato, garlic, lime juice and coriander (cilantro) and mash.

3 Turn the purée into a bowl and add the yogurt. Mix well.

4 Spoon the pâté into a serving dish and garnish with the chopped coriander (cilantro). Serve at once or leave to chill.

VARIATION

If you do not have a food processor or you would prefer to make a chunkier pâté, simply mash the ingredients with a fork.

COOK'S TIP

To make Melba toast, toast ready-sliced white or brown bread lightly on both sides under a preheated high grill (broiler) and remove the crusts. Holding the bread flat, slide a sharp knife between the toasted bread to split it horizontally. Cut into triangles and toast the untoasted side until the edges curl.

1

2

3

Smoked Fish & Potato Pâté

Serves 4

INGREDIENTS

650 g/$1\frac{1}{2}$ lb floury (mealy) potatoes, diced
300 g/$10\frac{1}{2}$ oz smoked mackerel, skinned and flaked
75 g/$2\frac{3}{4}$ oz cooked gooseberries
2 tsp lemon juice
2 tbsp crème fraîche
1 tbsp capers
1 gherkin, chopped
1 tbsp chopped dill pickle
1 tbsp chopped fresh dill
salt and pepper
lemon wedges, to garnish

1 Cook the diced potatoes in a saucepan of boiling water for 10 minutes until tender, then drain well.

2 Place the cooked potatoes in a food processor or blender.

3 Add the skinned and flaked smoked mackerel and process for 30 seconds until fairly smooth. Alternatively, mash with a fork.

4 Add the cooked gooseberries with the lemon juice and crème fraîche. Blend for a further 10 seconds or mash well.

5 Stir in the capers, gherkin, dill pickle and chopped fresh dill. Season well with salt and pepper.

6 Turn the fish pâté into a serving dish, garnish with lemon wedges and serve with slices of toast or warm crusty bread in chunks or slices.

COOK'S TIP

Use stewed, canned or bottled cooked gooseberries for convenience and to save time, or when fresh gooseberries are out of season.

VARIATION

Use other tart fruits, such as stewed apples, instead of the gooseberries if they are unavailable.

3

4

5

Potato Kibbeh

Serves 4

INGREDIENTS

175 g/6 oz bulgar wheat
350 g/12 oz floury (mealy) potatoes, diced
2 small eggs
25 g/1 oz/2 tbsp butter, melted
pinch of ground cumin
pinch of ground coriander
pinch of grated nutmeg
salt and pepper
oil for deep-frying

STUFFING:
175 g/6 oz minced lamb
1 small onion, chopped
1 tbsp pine kernels (nuts)
25 g/1 oz dried apricots, chopped
pinch of grated nutmeg
pinch of ground cinnamon
1 tbsp chopped fresh coriander (cilantro)
2 tbsp lamb stock

1 Put the bulgar wheat in a bowl and cover with boiling water. Soak for 30 minutes until the water has been absorbed and the bulgar wheat has swollen.

2 Meanwhile, cook the diced potatoes in a saucepan of boiling water for 10 minutes or until cooked through. Drain and mash until smooth.

3 Add the bulgar wheat to the mashed potato with the eggs, the melted butter, the ground cumin and coriander, and the grated nutmeg. Season well with salt and pepper.

4 To make the stuffing, dry fry the lamb for 5 minutes, add the onion and cook for a further 2–3 minutes. Add the remaining stuffing ingredients and cook for 5 minutes until the lamb stock has been absorbed. Leave the mixture to cool slightly, then divide into 8 portions. Roll each one into a ball.

5 Divide the potato mixture into 8 portions and flatten each into a round. Place a portion of stuffing in the centre of each round. Shape the coating around the stuffing to encase it completely.

6 In a large saucepan or deep fat fryer, heat the oil to 180°C–190°C/350°F–375°F or until a cube of bread browns in 30 seconds, and cook the kibbeh for 5–7 minutes until golden brown. Drain well and serve at once.

3

5

5

Potato & Meatballs in Spicy Sauce

Serves 4

INGREDIENTS

225 g/8 oz floury (mealy) potatoes, diced
225 g/8 oz minced beef or lamb
1 onion, finely chopped
1 tbsp chopped fresh coriander (cilantro)
1 celery stick, finely chopped
2 garlic cloves, crushed
25 g/1 oz/2 tbsp butter
1 tbsp vegetable oil
salt and pepper
chopped fresh coriander (cilantro), to garnish

SAUCE:
1 tbsp vegetable oil
1 onion, finely chopped
2 tsp soft brown sugar
400 g/14 oz can chopped tomatoes
1 green chilli, chopped
1 tsp paprika
150 ml/$^1/_4$ pint/$^2/_3$ cup vegetable stock
2 tsp cornflour (cornstarch)

1 Cook the diced potatoes in a saucepan of boiling water for 25 minutes until cooked through. Drain well and transfer to a large mixing bowl. Mash until smooth.

2 Add the minced beef or lamb, onion, coriander (cilantro), celery and garlic and mix well.

3 Bring the mixture together with your hands and roll it into 20 small balls.

4 To make the sauce, heat the oil in a pan and sauté the onion for 5 minutes. Add the remaining sauce ingredients and bring to the boil, stirring. Lower the heat and simmer for 20 minutes.

5 Meanwhile, heat the butter and oil for the potato and meat balls in a frying pan (skillet). Add the balls in batches and cook for 10–15 minutes until browned, turning frequently. Keep warm whilst cooking the remainder. Serve the potato and meatballs in a warm shallow ovenproof dish with the sauce poured around them and garnished with coriander (cilantro).

COOK'S TIP

Make the potato and meatballs in advance and chill or freeze them for later use. Make sure you defrost them thoroughly before cooking.

Potato & Fish Balls with Tomato Sauce

Serves 4

INGREDIENTS

450 g/1 lb floury (mealy) potatoes, diced
2 smoked fish fillets, such as cod, about 225 g/8 oz total weight, skinned
40 g/1½ oz/3 tbsp butter
2 eggs, beaten
1 tbsp chopped fresh dill
½ tsp cayenne pepper
oil for deep-frying
salt and pepper
dill sprigs, to garnish

SAUCE:
300 ml/½ pint/1¼ cups passata
1 tbsp tomato purée (paste)
2 tbsp chopped fresh dill
150 ml/¼ pint/⅔ cup fish stock

1 Cook the diced potatoes in a saucepan of boiling water for 10 minutes or until cooked. Drain well, then add the butter to the potato and mash until smooth. Season well with salt and pepper.

2 Meanwhile, poach the fish in boiling water for 10 minutes, turning once. Drain and mash the fish. Stir it into the potato mixture and leave to cool.

3 While the potato and fish mixture is cooling, make the sauce. Put the passata, tomato purée (paste), dill and stock in a pan and bring to the boil. Reduce the heat, cover the pan and simmer for 20 minutes until thickened.

4 Add the eggs, dill and cayenne pepper to the potato and fish mixture and beat until well mixed.

5 In a large saucepan or deep fat fryer, heat the oil to 180°C–190°C/350°F–375°F, or until a cube of bread browns in 30 seconds. Drop dessert spoons of the potato mixture into the oil and cook for 3–4 minutes until golden brown. Drain on paper towels.

6 Garnish the potato and fish balls with dill sprigs and serve with the tomato sauce.

VARIATION

Smoked fish is used for extra flavour, but white fish fillets or minced prawns (shrimp) may be used, if preferred.

Thai Potato Crab Cakes

Serves 4

INGREDIENTS

450 g/1 lb floury (mealy) potatoes, diced
175 g/6 oz white crab meat, drained if canned
4 spring onions (scallions), chopped
1 tsp light soy sauce
½ tsp sesame oil
1 tsp chopped lemon grass
1 tsp lime juice
3 tbsp plain (all-purpose) flour
2 tbsp vegetable oil
salt and pepper

SAUCE:
4 tbsp finely chopped cucumber
2 tbsp clear honey
1 tbsp garlic wine vinegar
½ tsp light soy sauce
1 red chilli, chopped

TO GARNISH:
1 red chilli, sliced
cucumber slices

1 Cook the diced potatoes in a saucepan of boiling water for 10 minutes until cooked through. Drain well and mash.

2 Mix the crab meat into the potato with the spring onions (scallions), soy sauce, sesame oil, lemon grass, lime juice and flour. Season with salt and pepper.

3 Divide the potato mixture into 8 portions of equal size and shape them into small rounds, using floured hands.

4 Heat the oil in a wok or frying pan (skillet) and cook the cakes, 4 at a time, for 5–7 minutes, turning once. Keep warm and repeat with the remaining cakes.

5 Meanwhile, make the sauce. In a small serving bowl, mix the cucumber, honey, vinegar, soy sauce and chopped red chilli.

6 Garnish the cakes with the sliced red chilli and cucumber slices and serve with the sauce.

COOK'S TIP

Do not make the cucumber sauce too far in advance as the water from the cucumber will make the sauce runny and dilute the flavour.

Potato & Mixed Mushroom Cakes

Serves 4

INGREDIENTS

450 g/1 lb floury (mealy) potatoes, diced
25 g/1 oz/2 tbsp butter
175 g/6 oz mixed mushrooms, chopped
2 garlic cloves, crushed
1 small egg, beaten
1 tbsp chopped fresh chives, plus extra to garnish
flour, for dusting
oil, for frying
salt and pepper

1 Cook the potatoes in a pan of boiling water for 10 minutes or until cooked through. Drain well, mash and set aside.

2 Meanwhile, melt the butter in a frying pan (skillet) and cook the mushrooms and garlic for 5 minutes, stirring. Drain well.

3 Stir the mushrooms and garlic into the potato together with the beaten egg and chives.

4 Divide the mixture equally into 4 portions and shape them into round cakes. Toss them in the flour until the outside of the cakes is completely coated.

5 Heat the oil in a frying pan (skillet) and cook the potato cakes over a medium heat for 10 minutes until they are golden brown, turning them over halfway through. Serve the cakes at once, with a simple crisp salad.

COOK'S TIP

Prepare the cakes in advance, cover and leave to chill in the refrigerator for up to 24 hours, if you wish.

VARIATION

If chives are unavailable, use other fresh herbs of your choice. Sage, tarragon and coriander (cilantro) all combine well with mixed mushrooms.

Potato, Cheese & Onion Rosti

Serves 4

INGREDIENTS

900 g/2 lb Maris Piper potatoes
1 onion, grated
50 g/2 oz Gruyère cheese, grated
2 tbsp chopped fresh parsley

1 tbsp olive oil
25 g/1 oz/2 tbsp butter
salt and pepper

TO GARNISH:
shredded spring onion (scallion)
1 small tomato, quartered

1 Parboil the potatoes in a pan of boiling water for 10 minutes and leave to cool. Peel the potatoes and grate with a coarse grater. Place the grated potatoes in a large mixing bowl.

2 Stir in the onion, cheese and parsley. Season well with salt and pepper. Divide the potato mixture into 4 portions of equal size and form them into cakes.

3 Heat half of the olive oil and butter in a frying pan (skillet) and cook 2 of the potato cakes over a high heat for 1 minute, then reduce the heat and cook for 5 minutes until they are golden underneath. Turn them over and cook for a further 5 minutes.

4 Repeat with the other half of the oil and butter to cook the remaining 2 cakes. Transfer to serving plates, garnish and serve.

COOK'S TIP

The potato cakes should be flattened as much as possible during cooking, otherwise the outside will be cooked before the centre.

VARIATION

To make these rosti into a more substantial meal, add chopped cooked bacon or ham to the potato mixture.

Potato & Cauliflower Fritters

Serves 4

INGREDIENTS

225 g/8 oz floury (mealy) potatoes, diced
225 g/8 oz cauliflower florets
2 tbsp grated Parmesan cheese
1 egg
1 egg white for coating
oil, for frying
paprika, for dusting (optional)
salt and pepper
crispy bacon slices, chopped, to serve

1 Cook the potatoes in a saucepan of boiling water for 10 minutes until cooked through. Drain well and mash.

2 Cook the cauliflower florets in a separate pan of boiling water for 10 minutes.

3 Drain the cauliflower florets and mix into the mashed potato. Stir in the grated Parmesan cheese and season well with salt and pepper.

4 Separate the whole egg and beat the yolk into the potato and cauliflower, mixing well.

5 Lightly whisk both the egg whites in a clean bowl, then carefully fold into the potato and cauliflower mixture.

6 Divide the potato mixture into 8 equal portions and shape them into rounds.

7 Heat the oil in a frying pan (skillet) and cook the fritters for 3–5 minutes, turning once halfway through cooking.

8 Dust the cooked fritters with a little paprika, if preferred, and serve at once accompanied by the crispy chopped bacon.

VARIATION

Any other vegetable, such as broccoli, can be used in this recipe instead of the cauliflower florets, if you prefer.

3

6

7

Potato Fritters with Garlic Sauce

Serves 4

INGREDIENTS

450 g/1 lb waxy potatoes, cut into large cubes
125 g/4½ oz Parmesan cheese, grated
oil, for deep-frying

SAUCE:
25 g/1 oz/2 tbsp butter
1 onion, halved and sliced
2 garlic cloves, crushed
25 g/1 oz/¼ cup plain (all-purpose) flour
300 ml/½ pint/1¼ cups milk
1 tbsp chopped fresh parsley

BATTER:
50 g/1¾ oz/½ cup plain (all-purpose) flour
1 small egg
150 ml/¼ pint/⅔ cup milk

1 To make the sauce, melt the butter in a saucepan and cook the sliced onion and garlic for 2–3 minutes. Add the flour and cook for 1 minute.

2 Remove from the heat and stir in the milk and parsley. Return to the heat and bring to the boil. Keep warm.

3 Meanwhile, cook the cubed potatoes in a saucepan of boiling water for 5–10 minutes until just firm. Do not overcook or they will fall apart.

4 Drain the potatoes and toss them in the Parmesan cheese.

5 To make the batter, place the flour in a mixing bowl and gradually beat in the egg and milk until smooth. Dip the potato cubes into the batter to coat them.

6 In a large saucepan or deep fat fryer, heat the oil to 180°–C190°C/ 350°F–375°F, or until a cube of bread browns in 30 seconds, and cook the fritters for 3–4 minutes or until golden. Drain the fritters with a perforated spoon and transfer them to a serving bowl. Serve with the sauce.

COOK'S TIP

Coat the potatoes in the Parmesan whilst still slightly wet to ensure that the cheese sticks and coats well.

4

5

6

Potato Croquettes with Ham & Cheese

Serves 4

INGREDIENTS

450 g/1 lb floury (mealy) potatoes, diced
300 ml/½ pint/1½ cups milk
25 g/1 oz/2 tbsp butter
4 spring onions (scallions), chopped
75 g/2¾ oz Cheddar cheese
50 g/1¾ oz smoked ham, chopped
1 celery stick, diced
1 egg, beaten
50 g/1¾ oz/½ cup plain (all-purpose) flour
oil, for deep frying
salt and pepper

COATING:
2 eggs, beaten
125 g/4½ oz fresh wholemeal (whole wheat) breadcrumbs

SAUCE:
25 g/1 oz/2 tbsp butter
25 g/1 oz/ ¼ cup plain (all-purpose) flour
150 ml/¼ pint/⅔ cup milk
150 ml/¼ pint/⅔ cup vegetable stock
75 g/2⅔oz Cheddar cheese, grated
1 tsp Dijon mustard
1 tbsp chopped coriander (cilantro)

1 Place the potatoes in a pan with the milk and bring to the boil. Reduce to a simmer until the liquid has been absorbed and the potatoes are cooked.

2 Add the butter and mash the potatoes. Stir in the spring onions (scallions), cheese, ham, celery, egg and flour. Season and leave to cool.

3 To make the coating, whisk the eggs in a bowl. Put the breadcrumbs in a separate bowl.

4 Shape the potato mixture into 8 balls. First dip them in the egg, then in the breadcrumbs.

5 To make the sauce, melt the butter in a small pan. Add the flour and cook for 1 minute. Remove from the heat and stir in the milk, stock, cheese, mustard and herbs. Bring to the boil, stirring until thickened. Reduce the heat and keep warm.

6 In a deep fat fryer, heat the oil to 180°C–190°C/ 350°F–375°F and fry the croquettes for 5 minutes until golden. Drain well and serve with the sauce.

Hash Browns with Tomato Sauce

Serves 4

INGREDIENTS

450 g/1 lb waxy potatoes
1 carrot, diced
1 celery stick, diced
50 g/2 oz button mushrooms, diced
1 onion, diced
2 garlic cloves, crushed
25 g/1 oz frozen peas, thawed
50 g/2 oz Parmesan cheese, grated
4 tbsp vegetable oil
25 g/1 oz/2 tbsp butter
salt and pepper

SAUCE:
300 ml/½ pint/1¼ cups passata
2 tbsp chopped fresh coriander
1 tbsp Worcestershire sauce
½ tsp chilli powder
2 tsp brown sugar
2 tsp American mustard
85 ml/3 fl oz/⅓ cup vegetable stock

1 Cook the potatoes in a saucepan of boiling water for 10 minutes. Drain and leave to cool. Meanwhile, cook the carrot in boiling water for 5 minutes.

2 When cool, grate the potato with a coarse grater.

3 Drain the carrot and add it to the grated potato with the celery, mushrooms, onion, peas and cheese. Season well.

4 Place all of the sauce ingredients in a pan and bring to the boil. Reduce the heat and simmer for 15 minutes.

5 Divide the potato mixture into 8 portions of equal size and shape into flattened rectangles with your hands.

6 Heat the oil and butter in a frying pan (skillet) and cook the hash browns over a low heat for 4–5 minutes on each side until crisp and golden brown.

7 Serve the hash browns with the tomato sauce.

COOK'S TIP

Use any mixture of vegetables for this recipe. For a non-vegetarian dish, add bacon pieces or diced ham for added flavour.

3

4

5

Potato Pancakes with Soured Cream & Salmon

Serves 4

INGREDIENTS

450 g/1 lb floury (mealy) potatoes, grated
2 spring onions (scallions), chopped
2 tbsp self-raising flour
2 eggs, beaten
2 tbsp vegetable oil
salt and pepper
fresh chives, to garnish

TOPPING:
150 ml/¼ pint/⅔ cup soured cream
125 g/4½ oz smoked salmon

1 Rinse the grated potatoes under cold running water, drain and pat dry on paper towels. Transfer to a mixing bowl.

2 Mix the chopped spring onions (scallions), flour and eggs into the potatoes and season well with salt and pepper.

3 Heat 1 tbsp of the oil in a frying pan (skillet). Drop about 4 tablespoonfuls of the mixture into the pan and spread each one with the back of a spoon to form a round (the mixture should make 16 pancakes). Cook for 5–7 minutes, turning once, until golden. Drain well.

4 Heat the remaining oil and cook the remaining mixture in batches.

5 Top the pancakes with the soured cream and smoked salmon, garnish with fresh chives and serve hot.

COOK'S TIP

Smaller versions of this dish may be made and served as appetizers.

VARIATION

These pancakes are equally delicious topped with prosciutto or any other dry-cured ham instead of the smoked salmon.

2

3

3

Potato Omelette with Feta Cheese & Spinach

Serves 4

INGREDIENTS

75 g/3 oz/$^1/_3$ cup butter
6 waxy potatoes, diced
3 garlic cloves, crushed
1 tsp paprika
2 tomatoes, skinned, seeded and diced
12 eggs
pepper

FILLING:
225 g/8 oz baby spinach
1 tsp fennel seeds
125 g/4$^1/_2$ oz feta cheese, diced
4 tbsp natural yogurt

1 Heat 2 tbsp of the butter in a frying pan (skillet) and cook the potatoes over a low heat for 7–10 minutes until golden, stirring constantly. Transfer to a bowl.

2 Add the garlic, paprika and tomatoes and cook for a further 2 minutes.

3 Whisk the eggs together in a jug and season with pepper. Pour the eggs into the potatoes and mix well.

4 Place the spinach in boiling water for 1 minute until just wilted. Drain and refresh the spinach under cold running water and pat dry with paper towels. Stir in the fennel seeds, feta cheese and yogurt.

5 Heat 1 tbsp of the butter in a 15 cm/6 inch omelette or frying pan (skillet). Ladle a quarter of the egg and potato mixture into the pan. Cook for 2 minutes, turning once, until set.

6 Transfer the omelette to a serving plate. Spoon a quarter of the spinach mixture on to one half of the omelette, then fold the omelette in half over the filling. Repeat to make 4 omelettes.

VARIATION

Use any other cheese, such as blue cheese, instead of the feta and blanched broccoli in place of the baby spinach, if you prefer.

3

4

5

Spanish Tortilla

Serves 4

INGREDIENTS

1 kg/ 2.2 lb waxy potatoes, thinly sliced
4 tbsp vegetable oil
1 onion, sliced
2 garlic cloves, crushed
1 green (bell) pepper, diced
2 tomatoes, deseeded and chopped
25 g/1 oz canned sweetcorn, drained
6 large eggs, beaten
2 tbsp chopped fresh parsley
salt and pepper

1 Parboil the potatoes in a saucepan of boiling water for 5 minutes. Drain well.

2 Heat the oil in a large frying pan (skillet), add the potato and onions and sauté gently for 5 minutes, stirring constantly, until the potatoes have browned.

3 Add the garlic, diced (bell) pepper, chopped tomatoes and sweetcorn, mixing well.

4 Pour in the eggs and add the chopped parsley. Season well with salt and pepper. Cook for 10–12 minutes until the underside is cooked through.

5 Remove the frying pan (skillet) from the heat and continue to cook the tortilla under a preheated medium grill (broiler) for 5–7 minutes or until the tortilla is set and the top is golden brown.

6 Cut the tortilla into wedges or cubes, depending on your preference, and serve with salad. In Spain tortillas are served hot, cold or warm.

COOK'S TIP

Ensure that the handle of your pan is heatproof before placing it under the grill (broiler) and be sure to use an oven glove when removing it as it will be very hot.

2

3

4

Paprika Crisps

Serves 4

INGREDIENTS

2 large potatoes
3 tbsp olive oil
½ tsp paprika pepper
salt

1 Using a sharp knife, slice the potatoes very thinly so that they are almost transparent. Drain the potato slices thoroughly and pat dry with paper towels.

2 Heat the oil in a large frying pan (skillet) and add the paprika, stirring constantly, to ensure that the paprika doesn't catch and burn.

3 Add the potato slices to the frying pan (skillet) and cook them in a single layer for about 5 minutes or until the potato slices just begin to curl slightly at the edges.

4 Remove the potato slices from the pan using a perforated spoon and transfer them to paper towels to drain thoroughly.

5 Thread the potato slices on to several wooden kebab (kabob) skewers.

6 Sprinkle the potato slices with a little salt and cook over a medium hot barbecue (grill) or under a medium grill (broiler) for 10 minutes, turning frequently, until the potato slices begin to crispen. Sprinkle with a little more salt, if preferred, and serve.

VARIATION

You could use curry powder or any other spice to flavour the crisps instead of the paprika, if you prefer.

1

4
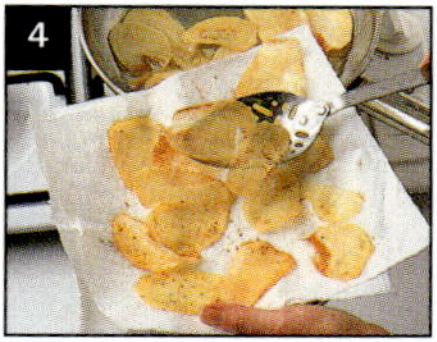

5

Creamy Mushrooms & Potatoes

Serves 4

INGREDIENTS

25 g/1 oz dried ceps
225 g/8 oz floury (mealy) potatoes, diced
25 g/1 oz/2 tbsp butter, melted
4 tbsp double (heavy) cream
2 tbsp chopped fresh chives
25 g/1 oz Emmental cheese, grated
8 large open capped mushrooms
150 ml/¼ pint/⅔ cup vegetable stock
salt and pepper
fresh chives, to garnish

1 Place the dried ceps in a bowl, cover with boiling water and leave to soak for 20 minutes.

2 Meanwhile, cook the potatoes in a saucepan of boiling water for 10 minutes until cooked. Drain well and mash.

3 Drain the soaked ceps and chop them finely. Mix them into the mashed potato.

4 Mix the butter, cream and chives together and pour into the cep and potato mixture. Season with salt and pepper.

5 Remove the stalks from the open-capped mushrooms. Chop the stalks and stir them into the potato mixture. Spoon the mixture into the open-capped mushrooms and sprinkle the cheese over the top.

6 Place the filled mushrooms in a shallow ovenproof dish and pour in the vegetable stock.

7 Cover the dish and cook in a preheated oven, 220°C/425°F/Gas Mark 7, for 20 minutes. Remove the lid and cook for 5 minutes until golden on top.

8 Garnish the mushrooms with fresh chives and serve at once.

VARIATION

Use fresh mushrooms instead of the dried ceps, if preferred, and stir a mixture of chopped nuts into the mushroom stuffing mixture for extra crunch.

Potato Noodles with Cheese, Mushrooms & Bacon

Serves 4

INGREDIENTS

450 g/1 lb floury (mealy) potatoes, diced
225 g/8 oz/2 cups plain (all-purpose) flour
1 egg, beaten
1 tbsp milk
salt and pepper
parsley sprig, to garnish

SAUCE:
1 tbsp vegetable oil
1 onion, chopped
1 garlic clove, crushed
125 g/4½ oz open-capped mushrooms, sliced
3 smoked bacon slices, chopped
50 g/2 oz Parmesan cheese, grated
300 ml/½ pint/1¼ cups double (heavy) cream
2 tbsp chopped fresh parsley

1 Cook the diced potatoes in a saucepan of boiling water for 10 minutes until cooked through. Drain well. Mash the potatoes until smooth, then beat in the flour, egg and milk. Season with salt and pepper and bring together to form a stiff paste.

2 On a lightly floured surface, roll out the paste to form a thin sausage shape. Cut the sausage into 2.5 cm/1 inch lengths. Bring a large pan of salted water to the boil, drop in the dough pieces and cook for 3–4 minutes. They will rise to the top when cooked.

3 To make the sauce, heat the oil in a pan and sauté the onion and garlic for 2 minutes. Add the mushrooms and bacon and cook for 5 minutes. Stir in the cheese, cream and parsley and season.

4 Drain the noodles and transfer to a warm pasta bowl. Spoon the sauce over the top and toss to mix. Garnish with a parsley sprig and serve.

COOK'S TIP

Make the dough in advance, then wrap and store the noodles in the refrigerator for up to 24 hours.

2

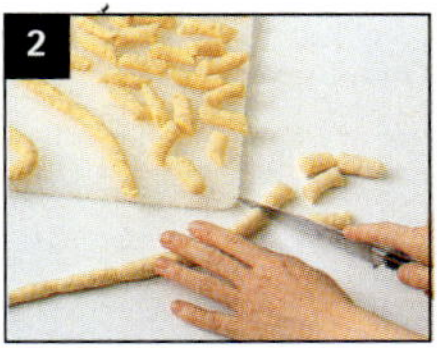
2

2

Potato & Mushroom Bake

Serves 4

INGREDIENTS

25 g/1 oz butter
450 g/1 lb waxy potatoes, thinly sliced
150 g/5 oz mixed mushrooms, sliced
1 tbsp chopped fresh rosemary
4 tbsp chopped fresh chives
2 garlic cloves, crushed
150 ml/¼ pint/⅔ cup double (heavy) cream
salt and pepper
fresh chives, to garnish

1 Grease a shallow round ovenproof dish with butter.

2 Parboil the sliced potatoes in a saucepan of boiling water for 10 minutes. Drain well. Layer a quarter of the potatoes in the base of the dish.

3 Arrange a quarter of the mushrooms on top of the potatoes and sprinkle with a quarter of the rosemary, chives and garlic.

4 Continue layering in the same order, finishing with a layer of potatoes on top.

5 Pour the cream over the top of the potatoes. Season well.

6 Cook in a preheated oven, 190°C/375°F/Gas Mark 5, for 45 minutes or until the bake is golden brown.

7 Garnish with fresh chives and serve at once.

COOK'S TIP

For a special occasion, the bake may be made in a lined cake tin (pan) and turned out to serve.

VARIATION

Use 50 g/2 oz re-hydrated dried mushrooms instead of the fresh mixed mushrooms, for a really intense flavour.

Spicy Potato-Filled Naan Breads

Serves 4

INGREDIENTS

225 g/8 oz waxy potatoes, scrubbed and diced
1 tbsp vegetable oil
1 onion, chopped
2 garlic cloves, crushed
1 tsp ground cumin
1 tsp ground coriander
½ tsp chilli powder
1 tbsp tomato purée (paste)
3 tbsp vegetable stock
75 g/2¾ oz baby spinach, shredded
4 small or 2 large naan breads
lime pickle, to serve

RAITHA:
150 ml/¼ pint/⅔ cup natural yogurt
4 tbsp diced cucumber
1 tbsp chopped mint

1 Cook the diced potatoes in a saucepan of boiling water for 10 minutes. Drain thoroughly.

2 Heat the vegetable oil in a separate saucepan and cook the onion and garlic for 3 minutes, stirring. Add the spices and cook for a further 2 minutes.

3 Stir in the potatoes, tomato purée (paste), vegetable stock and spinach. Cook for 5 minutes until the potatoes are tender.

4 Warm the naan breads in a preheated oven, 150°C/300°F/Gas Mark 2, for about 2 minutes.

5 To make the raitha, mix the yogurt, cucumber and mint together in a small bowl.

6 Remove the naan breads from the oven. Using a sharp knife, cut a pocket in the side of each naan bread. Spoon the spicy potato mixture into each pocket.

7 Serve the filled naan breads at once, accompanied by the raitha and lime pickle.

COOK'S TIP

To give the raitha a much stronger flavour, make it in advance and leave to chill in the refrigerator until ready to serve.

3

6

6

Potato & Spinach Filo Triangles

Serves 4

INGREDIENTS

225 g/8 oz waxy potatoes, diced finely
450 g/1 lb baby spinach
1 tomato, seeded and chopped
¼ tsp chilli powder
½ tsp lemon juice
225 g/8 oz packet filo pastry, thawed if frozen
25 g/1 oz butter, melted
salt and pepper

MAYONNAISE:
150 ml/¼ pint/⅔ cup mayonnaise
2 tsp lemon juice
rind of 1 lemon

1 Lightly grease a baking (cookie) sheet with a little butter.

2 Cook the potatoes in a saucepan of boiling water for 10 minutes or until cooked through. Drain thoroughly and place in a mixing bowl.

3 Meanwhile, put the spinach in a saucepan with 2 tbsp of water, cover and cook over a low heat for 2 minutes until wilted. Drain the spinach thoroughly and add to the potato.

4 Stir in the chopped tomato, chilli powder and lemon juice. Season to taste with salt and pepper.

5 Lightly butter 8 sheets of filo pastry. Spread out 4 of the sheets and lay the other 4 on top of each. Cut them into 20 x 10 cm/ 8 x 4 inch rectangles.

6 Spoon the potato and spinach mixture on to one end of each rectangle. Fold a corner of the pastry over the filling, fold the pointed end back over the pastry strip, then fold over the remaining pastry to form a triangle.

7 Place the triangles on the baking (cookie) sheet and bake in a preheated oven, 190°C/375°F/Gas Mark 5, for 20 minutes or until golden brown.

8 To make the mayonnaise, mix the mayonnaise, lemon juice and lemon rind together in a small bowl. Serve the potato and spinach filo triangles warm or cold with the lemon mayonnaise and a crisp green salad.

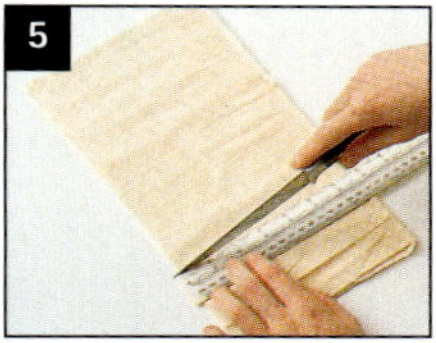

Side Dishes

When the potato is thought of as a component of a meal, it is inevitably associated with meat and vegetables, and is served either roasted or boiled. In fact, the potato is so versatile in its ability to combine with other flavourings and be cooked in so many different ways that it is the perfect base for a whole variety of delicious side dishes. This chapter demonstrates that versatility with a wide range of tantalising recipes.

Potatoes can be cooked and served in many different ways, such as mashing, roasting, stir-frying, pan-frying, deep-frying, baking and boiling. You will find all kinds of different recipes for side dishes in this chapter, including Candied Sweet Potatoes, Spanish Potatoes, Thai Potato Stir-fry and Steamed Potatoes En Papillotes. There are also classic recipes, such as Potatoes Dauphinois and Pommes Anna, as well as updated versions of traditional dishes, such as Chilli Roast Potatoes and Spicy Potato Fries. The variety is endless!

Colcannon

Serves 4

INGREDIENTS

225 g/8 oz green cabbage, shredded
85 ml/3 fl oz/$^1/_3$ cup milk
25 g/8 oz floury (mealy) potatoes, diced
1 large leek, chopped
pinch of grated nutmeg
15 g/$^1/_2$ oz/1 tbsp butter, melted
salt and pepper

1 Cook the shredded cabbage in a saucepan of boiling salted water for 7–10 minutes. Drain thoroughly and set aside.

2 Meanwhile, in a separate saucepan, bring the milk to the boil and add the potatoes and leek. Reduce the heat and simmer for 15–20 minutes or until they are cooked through.

3 Stir in the grated nutmeg and mash the potatoes and leeks together.

4 Add the drained cabbage to the potatoes and mix well.

5 Spoon the potato and cabbage mixture into a serving dish, making a hollow in the centre with the back of a spoon.

6 Pour the melted butter into the hollow and serve the dish immediately.

VARIATION

Add diced cooked bacon to the recipe for extra flavour, adding it with the leeks and cabbage.

COOK'S TIP

There are many different varieties of cabbage, which produce hearts at varying times of year, so you can be sure of being able to make this delicious cabbage dish all year round.

Candied Sweet Potatoes

Serves 4

INGREDIENTS

- 675 g/1 1/2 lb sweet potatoes, sliced
- 40 g/1 1/2 oz/3 tbsp butter
- 1 tbsp lime juice
- 75 g/2 3/4 oz/1/2 cup soft dark brown sugar
- 1 tbsp brandy
- grated rind of 1 lime
- lime wedges, to garnish

1 Cook the sweet potatoes in a saucepan of boiling water for 5 minutes. Test the potatoes have softened by pricking with a fork. Remove the sweet potatoes with a perforated spoon and drain thoroughly.

2 Melt the butter in a large frying pan (skillet). Add the lime juice and brown sugar and heat gently to dissolve the sugar.

3 Stir the sweet potatoes and the brandy into the sugar and lime juice mixture. Cook over a low heat for 10 minutes until the potato slices are cooked through.

4 Sprinkle the lime rind over the top of the sweet potatoes and mix well.

5 Transfer the candied sweet potatoes to a serving plate. Garnish with lime wedges and serve at once.

VARIATION

Serve this dish with spicy meats to complement the sweetness of the potatoes, if you prefer.

COOK'S TIP

Sweet potatoes have a pinkish skin and either white, yellow or orange flesh. It doesn't matter which type is used for this dish.

VARIATION

This dish may be prepared with waxy potatoes instead of sweet potatoes, if you prefer. Cook the potatoes for 10 minutes in step 1, instead of 5 minutes. Follow the same cooking method.

Potatoes with Onion & Herbs

Serves 4

INGREDIENTS

900 g/2 lb waxy potatoes, cut into cubes
125 g/4½ oz/½ cup butter
1 red onion, cut into 8
2 garlic cloves, crushed
1 tsp lemon juice
2 tbsp chopped fresh thyme
salt and pepper

1 Cook the cubed potatoes in a saucepan of boiling water for 10 minutes. Drain thoroughly.

2 Melt the butter in a large, heavy-based frying pan (skillet) and add the red onion wedges, garlic and lemon juice. Cook for 2–3 minutes, stirring.

3 Add the potatoes to the pan and mix well to coat in the butter mixture.

4 Reduce the heat, cover the frying pan (skillet) and cook for 25–30 minutes or until the potatoes are golden and tender.

5 Sprinkle the chopped thyme over the top of the potatoes and season with salt and pepper to taste.

6 Serve immediately as a side dish to accompany grilled meats or fish.

COOK'S TIP

Keep checking the potatoes and stirring throughout the cooking time to ensure that they do not burn or stick to the bottom of the frying pan (skillet).

COOK'S TIP

Onions are used in a multitude of dishes to which they add their pungent flavour. The beautifully coloured purple-red onions used here have a mild, slightly sweet flavour as well as looking extremely attractive. Because of their mild taste, they are equally good eaten raw in salads.

Caramelised New Potatoes

Serves 4

INGREDIENTS

675 g/1½ lb new potatoes, scrubbed
4 tbsp soft dark brown sugar
60 g/2 oz/½ cup butter
1 tbsp orange juice
1 tbsp chopped fresh parsley or coriander (cilantro)
salt and pepper
orange rind curls, to garnish

1 Cook the new potatoes in a saucepan of boiling water for 10 minutes or until almost tender. Drain thoroughly.

2 Melt the sugar in a large, heavy-based frying pan (skillet) over a low heat, stirring.

3 Add the butter and orange juice to the pan, stirring the mixture as the butter melts.

4 Add the potatoes to the orange and butter mixture and continue to cook, turning the potatoes frequently until they are completely coated in the caramel.

5 Sprinkle the chopped parsley or coriander (cilantro) over the potatoes and season to taste with salt and pepper.

6 Transfer the caramelised new potatoes to a serving dish and garnish with the orange rind. Serve immediately.

VARIATION

Lemon or lime juices may be used instead of the orange juce, if preferred. In addition, garnish the finished dish with pared lemon or lime rind, if preferred.

COOK'S TIP

Heat the sugar and butter gently, stirring constantly, to make sure that the mixture doesn't burn or stick to the bottom of the frying pan (skillet).

Spanish Potatoes

Serves 4

INGREDIENTS

2 tbsp olive oil
450 g/1 lb small new potatoes, halved
1 onion, halved and sliced
1 green (bell) pepper, cut into strips
1 tsp chilli powder
1 tsp prepared mustard
300 ml/½ pint/1¼ cups passata
300 ml/½ pint/1¼ cups vegetable stock
salt and pepper
chopped fresh parsley, to garnish

1 Heat the olive oil in a frying pan (skillet) and add the halved new potatoes and the sliced onion. Cook for 4–5 minutes, stirring frequently, until the onion slices have just softened.

2 Add the green (bell) pepper strips, chilli powder and mustard to the pan and cook for a further 2–3 minutes.

3 Stir the passata and the vegetable stock into the pan and bring to the boil. Reduce the heat and cook the mixture for about 25 minutes or until the potatoes are tender.

4 Transfer the potatoes to a serving dish. Sprinkle the parsley over the top of the potatoes and serve hot. Alternatively, leave the Spanish potatoes to cool completely and serve cold.

COOK'S TIP

In Spain, tapas are traditionally served with a glass of chilled sherry or some other aperitif.

COOK'S TIP

The array of little appetizer snacks known as tapas are a traditional Spanish social custom. Spaniards often visit several bars throughout the evening eating different tapas, ranging from stuffed olives and salted almonds, to slices of ham and deep-fried squid rings.

Spicy Indian Potatoes with Spinach

Serves 4

INGREDIENTS

½ tsp coriander seeds
1 tsp cumin seeds
4 tbsp vegetable oil
2 cardamon pods
1 cm/½ inch piece ginger root, grated
1 red chilli, chopped
1 onion, chopped
2 garlic cloves, crushed
450 g/1 lb new potatoes, quartered
675 g/1½ lb spinach, chopped
150 ml/¼ pint/⅔ cup vegetable stock
4 tbsp natural yogurt
salt

1 Grind the coriander and cumin seeds using a pestle and mortar.

2 Heat the oil in a frying pan (skillet). Add the ground coriander and cumin seeds to the pan together with the cardamom pods and ginger and cook for about 2 minutes.

3 Add the chopped chilli, onion and garlic to the pan. Cook for a further 2 minutes, stirring frequently

4 Add the potatoes to the pan together with the vegetable stock. Cook gently for 30 minutes or until the potatoes are cooked through, stirring occasionally.

5 Add the spinach to the pan and cook for a further 5 minutes.

6 Remove the pan from the heat and stir in the yogurt. Season with salt and pepper to taste. Transfer the potatoes and spinach to a serving dish and serve.

COOK'S TIP

This spicy dish is ideal served with a meat curry or alternatively, as part of a vegetarian meal.

VARIATION

Use frozen spinach instead of fresh spinach, if you prefer. Defrost the frozen spinach and drain it thoroughly before adding it to the dish, otherwise it will turn soggy.

Potatoes & Mushrooms in Red Wine

Serves 4

INGREDIENTS

125 g/4½ oz/½ cup butter
450 g/1 lb new potatoes, halved
200 ml/7 fl oz/¾ cup red wine
85 ml/3 fl oz/⅓ cup beef stock
8 shallots, halved
125 g/4½ oz oyster mushrooms
1 tbsp chopped fresh sage or coriander (cilantro)
salt and pepper
sage leaves or coriander (cilantro) sprigs, to garnish

1 Melt the butter in a heavy-based frying pan (skillet) and add the halved potatoes. Cook gently for 5 minutes, stirring constantly.

2 Add the red wine, beef stock and halved shallots. Season to taste with salt and pepper and then simmer for 30 minutes.

3 Stir in the mushrooms and chopped sage or coriander (cilantro) and cook for 5 minutes.

4 Turn the potatoes and mushrooms into a warm serving dish. Garnish with sage leaves or coriander (cilantro) sprigs and serve at once.

VARIATION

If oyster mushrooms are unavailable, other mushrooms, such as large open cap mushrooms, can be used instead.

COOK'S TIP

Oyster mushrooms may be grey, yellow or red in colour. They have a soft, melting texture and mild flavour. As they cook, they emit a lot of liquid and shrink to about half their original size. They require little cooking before they start to turn mushy, so add them at the end of the cooking time.

Gingered Potatoes

Serves 4

INGREDIENTS

675 g/1$^{1}/_{2}$ lb waxy potatoes, cubed
2 tbsp vegetable oil
5 cm/2 inch piece ginger root, grated
1 green chilli, chopped
1 celery stick, chopped
25 g/1 oz cashew nuts
few strands of saffron
3 tbsp boiling water
60 g/2 oz/$^{1}/_{4}$ cup butter
celery leaves, to garnish

1 Cook the potatoes in a saucepan of boiling water for 10 minutes. Drain thoroughly.

2 Heat the oil in a heavy-based frying pan (skillet) and add the potatoes. Cook for 3–4 minutes, stirring constantly.

3 Add the grated ginger, chilli, celery and cashew nuts and cook for 1 minute.

4 Meanwhile, place the saffron strands in a small bowl. Add the boiling water and leave to soak.

5 Add the butter to the pan and stir in the saffron mixture. Cook gently for 10 minutes or until the potatoes are tender.

6 Garnish the gingered potatoes with the celery leaves and serve at once.

VARIATION

If you prefer a less spicy dish, deseed the chopped green chilli or omit the chilli altogether.

COOK'S TIP

Use a non-stick, heavy-based frying pan (skillet) as the potato mixture is fairly dry and may stick to an ordinary pan.

Thai Potato Stir-Fry

Serves 4

INGREDIENTS

4 waxy potatoes, diced
2 tbsp vegetable oil
1 yellow (bell) pepper, diced
1 red (bell) pepper, diced
1 carrot, cut into matchstick strips
1 courgette (zucchini), cut into matchstick strips
2 garlic cloves, crushed
1 red chilli, sliced
1 bunch spring onions (scallions), halved lengthways
8 tbsp coconut milk
1 tsp chopped lemon grass
2 tsp lime juice
finely grated rind of 1 lime
1 tbsp chopped fresh coriander (cilantro)

1 Cook the diced potatoes in a saucepan of boiling water for 5 minutes. Drain thoroughly.

2 Heat the oil in a wok or large frying pan (skillet) and add the potatoes, diced (bell) peppers, carrot, courgette (zucchini), garlic and chilli. Stir-fry the vegetables for 2–3 minutes.

3 Stir in the spring onions, (scallions), coconut milk, chopped lemon grass and lime juice and stir-fry the mixture for a further 5 minutes.

4 Add the lime rind and coriander (cilantro) and stir-fry for 1 minute. Serve hot.

COOK'S TIP

Check that the potatoes are not overcooked in step 1, otherwise the potato pieces will disintegrate when they are stir-fried in the wok.

VARIATION

Almost any combination of vegetables is suitable for this dish; the yellow and red (bell) peppers, for example, can be replaced with crisp green beans or mangetout (snow peas).

Cheese & Potato Slices

Serves 4

INGREDIENTS

3 large waxy potatoes, unpeeled and thickly sliced
16 tbsp fresh white breadcrumbs
8 tbsp grated Parmesan cheese
1½ tsp chilli powder
2 eggs, beaten
oil, for deep frying
chilli powder, for dusting (optional)

1 Cook the sliced potatoes in a saucepan of boiling water for 10–15 minutes or until the potatoes are just tender. Drain thoroughly.

2 Mix the breadcrumbs, cheese and chilli powder together in a bowl then transfer to a shallow dish. Pour the beaten eggs into a separate shallow dish.

3 Dip the potato slices in egg and then roll them in the breadcrumbs to coat completely.

4 Heat the oil in a large saucepan or deep fat fryer to 180°C–190°C/350°F -375°F, or until a cube of bread browns in 30 seconds. Cook the cheese and potato slices, in several batches, for 4–5 minutes or until a golden brown colour.

5 Remove the cheese and potato slices with a perforated spoon and leave to drain thoroughly on paper towels. Keep the cheese and potato slices warm while you cook the remaining batches.

6 Transfer the cheese and potato slices to warm serving plates. Dust with chilli powder, if using, and serve immediately.

VARIATION

For a healthy alternative, use fresh wholemeal (whole wheat) breadcrumbs instead of the white ones used here, if you prefer.

COOK'S TIP

The cheese and potato slices may be coated in the breadcrumb mixture in advance and then stored in the refrigerator until ready to use.

Grilled Potatoes with Lime Mayonnaise

Serves 4

INGREDIENTS

450 g/1 lb potatoes, unpeeled and scrubbed
40 g/1½ oz/3 tbsp butter, melted
2 tbsp chopped fresh thyme
paprika, for dusting

LIME MAYONNAISE:
150 ml/¼ pint/⅔ cup mayonnaise
2 tsp lime juice
finely grated rind of 1 lime
1 garlic clove, crushed
pinch of paprika
salt and pepper

1 Cut the potatoes into 1 cm/½ inch thick slices.

2 Cook the potatoes in a saucepan of boiling water for 5–7 minutes – they should still be quite firm. Remove the potatoes with a perforated spoon and drain thoroughly.

3 Line a grill (broiler) pan with kitchen foil. Place the potato slices on top of the foil.

4 Brush the potatoes with the melted butter and sprinkle the chopped thyme on top. Season to taste with salt and pepper.

5 Cook the potatoes under a preheated medium heat for 10 minutes, turning once.

6 Meanwhile, make the lime mayonnaise. Combine the mayonnaise, lime juice, lime rind, garlic, paprika and salt and pepper to taste in a bowl.

7 Dust the hot potato slices with a little paprika and serve with the lime mayonnaise.

COOK'S TIP

For an impressive side dish, thread the potato slices on to skewers and cook over medium hot barbecue coals.

VARIATION

The lime mayonnaise may be spooned over the grilled (broiled) potatoes to coat them just before serving, if you prefer.

3

4

6

Trio of Potato Purées

Serves 4

INGREDIENTS

300 g/10½ oz floury (mealy) potatoes, chopped
125 g/4½ oz swede, chopped
1 carrot, chopped
450 g/1 lb spinach
1 tbsp milk
15 g/½ oz/1 tbsp butter
25 g/1 oz/¼ cup plain (all purpose) flour
1 egg
½ tsp ground cinnamon
1 tbsp orange juice
¼ tsp grated nutmeg
salt and pepper
carrot matchsticks, to garnish

1 Lightly grease four 150 ml/¼ pint/⅔ cup ramekins or mini pudding basins.

2 Cook the potatoes in a saucepan of boiling water for 10 minutes. Meanwhile, in separate pans cook the swede and carrot in boiling water for 10 minutes. Blanch the spinach in a little boiling water for 5 minutes. Drain all of the vegetables.

3 Add the milk and butter to the potatoes and mash until smooth. Stir in the flour and egg.

4 Divide the potato mixture into 3 equal portions and place in 3 separate bowls. Spoon the swede into one bowl and mix well. Spoon the carrot into the second bowl and mix well. Spoon the spinach into the third bowl and mix well.

5 Add the cinnamon to the swede and potato mixture and season with salt and pepper to taste. Stir the orange juice into the carrot and potato mixture. Stir the nutmeg into the spinach and potato mixture.

6 Spoon a layer of the swede and potato mixture into each of the ramekins or basins and smooth over the top. Cover each with a layer of spinach and potato mixture, then top with the carrot and potato mixture. Cover the ramekins with foil and place in a roasting tin (pan). Half fill the tin (pan) with boiling water and cook in a preheated oven, 180°C/350°F/Gas Mark 4, for 40 minutes or until set.

7 Turn out on to serving plates, garnish with the carrot matchsticks and serve at once.

Spicy Potato Fries

Serves 4

INGREDIENTS

4 large waxy potatoes
2 sweet potatoes
50 g/1$^3/_4$ oz/4 tbsp butter, melted
$^1/_2$ tsp chilli powder
1 tsp garam masala
salt

1 Cut the potatoes and sweet potatoes into slices about 1 cm/$^1/_2$ inch thick, then cut them into chip shapes.

2 Place the potatoes in a large bowl of cold salted water. Leave to soak for 20 minutes.

3 Remove the potato slices with a perforated spoon and drain thoroughly. Pat with paper towels until completely dry.

4 Pour the melted butter on to a baking (cookie) sheet. Transfer the potato slices to the baking (cookie) sheet. Sprinkle with the chilli powder and garam masala, turning the potato slices to coat them with the mixture.

5 Cook the chips in a preheated oven, 200°C/ 400°F/Gas Mark 6, for 40 minutes, turning frequently until browned and cooked through.

6 Drain the chips on paper towels to remove the excess oil and serve at once.

COOK'S TIP

Rinsing the potatoes in cold water before cooking removes the starch, thus preventing them from sticking together. Soaking the potatoes in a bowl of cold salted water actually makes the cooked chips crisper.

VARIATION

For added flavour, sprinkle the chips with fennel seeds or cumin seeds, before serving.

Italian Potato Wedges

Serves 4

INGREDIENTS

2 large waxy potatoes, unpeeled
4 large ripe tomatoes, peeled and seeded
150 ml/¼ pint/⅔ cup vegetable stock
2 tbsp tomato purée (paste)
1 small yellow (bell) pepper, cut into strips
125 g/4½ oz button mushrooms, quartered
1 tbsp chopped fresh basil
50 g/1¾ oz cheese, grated
salt and pepper

1 Cut each of the potatoes into 8 equal wedges. Parboil the potatoes in a pan of boiling water for 15 minutes. Drain well and place in a shallow ovenproof dish.

2 Chop the tomatoes and add to the dish. Mix together the vegetable stock and tomato purée (paste), then pour the mixture over the potatoes and tomatoes.

3 Add the yellow (bell) pepper strips, quartered mushrooms and chopped basil. Season well with salt and pepper.

4 Sprinkle the grated cheese over the top and cook in a preheated oven, 190°C/375°F/Gas Mark 5, for 15–20 minutes until the topping is golden brown. Serve at once.

COOK'S TIP

For the topping, use any cheese that melts well, such as Mozzarella, the traditional pizza cheese. Alternatively, you could use either Gruyère or Emmental cheese, if you prefer.

VARIATION

These potato wedges can also be served as a light supper dish, accompanied by chunks of crusty, fresh brown or white bread.

Saffron-Flavoured Potatoes with Mustard

Serves 4

INGREDIENTS

1 tsp saffron strands
6 tbsp boiling water
675 g/1½ lb waxy potatoes, unpeeled and cut into wedges
1 red onion, cut into 8 wedges
2 garlic cloves, crushed
1 tbsp white wine vinegar
2 tbsp olive oil
1 tbsp wholegrain mustard
5 tbsp vegetable stock
5 tbsp dry white wine
2 tsp chopped fresh rosemary
salt and pepper

1 Place the saffron strands in a small bowl and pour over the boiling water. Leave to soak for about 10 minutes.

2 Place the potatoes in a roasting tin (pan) together with the red onion wedges and crushed garlic.

3 Add the vinegar, oil, mustard, vegetable stock, white wine, rosemary and saffron water to the potatoes and onion in the tin (pan). Season to taste with salt and pepper.

4 Cover the roasting tin (pan) with kitchen foil and bake in a preheated oven, 200°C/400°F/Gas Mark 6, for 30 minutes.

5 Remove the foil and cook the potatoes for a further 10 minutes until crisp, browned and cooked through. Serve hot.

VARIATION

If preferred, use only wine to flavour the potatoes rather than a mixture of wine and stock.

COOK'S TIP

Turmeric may be used instead of saffron to provide the yellow colour in this recipe. However, it is worth using saffron, if possible, for the lovely nutty flavour it gives a dish.

2

3

5

Chilli Roast Potatoes

Serves 4

INGREDIENTS

450 g/1 lb small new potatoes, scrubbed
150 ml/¼ pint/⅔ cup vegetable oil
1 tsp chilli powder
½ tsp caraway seeds
1 tsp salt
1 tbsp chopped fresh basil

1 Cook the potatoes in a saucepan of boiling water for 10 minutes. Drain thoroughly.

2 Pour a little of the oil into a shallow roasting tin (pan) to coat the bottom of the tin (pan). Heat the oil in a preheated oven, 200°C/400°F/Gas Mark 6, for 10 minutes. Add the potatoes to the tin (pan) and brush them with the hot oil.

3 In a small bowl, mix together the chilli powder, caraway seeds and salt. Sprinkle the mixture over the potatoes, turning to coat them all over.

4 Add the remaining oil to the tin (pan) and roast in the oven for about 15 minutes or until the potatoes are cooked through.

5 Using a perforated spoon, remove the potatoes from the the oil, and transfer them to a warm serving dish. Sprinkle the chopped basil over the top and serve immediately.

COOK'S TIP

These spicy potatoes are ideal for serving with plain meat dishes, such as roasted or grilled lamb, pork or chicken.

VARIATION

Use any other spice of your choice, such as curry powder or paprika, for a variation in flavour.

Parmesan Potatoes

Serves 4

INGREDIENTS

6 potatoes
50 g/1¾ oz Parmesan cheese, grated
pinch of grated nutmeg
4 smoked bacon slices, cut into strips
1 tbsp chopped fresh parsley
oil, for roasting
salt

1 Cut the potatoes in half lengthways and cook them in a saucepan of boiling salted water for 10 minutes. Drain thoroughly.

2 Mix the grated Parmesan cheese, nutmeg and parsley together in a shallow bowl.

3 Roll the potato pieces in the cheese mixture to coat them completely. Shake off any excess.

4 Pour a little oil into a roasting tin (pan) and heat it in a preheated oven, 200°C/400°F/Gas Mark 6, for 10 minutes. Remove from the oven and place the potatoes into the tin (pan). Return the tin (pan) to the oven and cook for 30 minutes, turning once.

5 Remove from the oven and sprinkle the bacon on top of the potatoes. Return to the oven for 15 minutes or until the potatoes and bacon are cooked. Drain off any excess fat and serve.

COOK'S TIP

Parmesan cheese has been used for its distinctive flavour, but any finely grated hard cheese would be suitable for this dish.

VARIATION

If you prefer, use slices of salami or Parma ham instead of the bacon, adding it to the dish 5 minutes before the end of the cooking time.

3

4

5

Potatoes Dauphinois

Serves 4

INGREDIENTS

15 g/½ oz/1 tbsp butter
675 g/1½ lb waxy potatoes, sliced
2 garlic cloves, crushed
1 red onion, sliced
75 g/3 oz Gruyère cheese, grated
300 ml/½ pint/1¼ cups double (heavy) cream
salt and pepper

1 Lightly grease a 1 litre/1¾ pint/4 cup shallow ovenproof dish with a little butter.

2 Arrange a single layer of potato slices in the base of the prepared dish.

3 Top the potato slices with a little of the garlic, sliced red onion and grated Gruyére cheese. Season to taste with a little salt and pepper.

4 Repeat the layers in exactly the same order, finishing with a layer of potatoes topped with cheese.

5 Pour the cream over the top of the potatoes and cook in a preheated oven, 180°C/350°F/Gas Mark 4, for 1½ hours or until the potatoes are cooked through, browned and crispy. Serve at once.

COOK'S TIP

Add a layer of chopped bacon or ham to this dish, if you prefer, and serve with a crisp green salad for a light supper.

VARIATION

There are many versions of this classic potato dish, but the different recipes always contain double (heavy) cream, making it a rich and very filling side dish or accompaniment. This recipe must be cooked in a shallow dish to ensure there is plenty of crispy topping.

Pommes Anna

Serves 4

INGREDIENTS

60 g/2 oz/¼ cup butter, melted
675 g/1½ lb waxy potatoes
4 tbsp chopped mixed fresh herbs
salt and pepper
chopped fresh herbs, to garnish

1 Brush a shallow 1 litre/1¾ pint/4 cup ovenproof dish with a little of the melted butter.

2 Slice the potatoes thinly and pat dry with paper towels.

3 Arrange a layer of potato slices in the prepared dish until the base is covered. Brush with a little butter and sprinkle with a quarter of the chopped mixed herbs. Season to taste.

4 Continue layering the potato slices, brushing each layer with melted butter and sprinkling with herbs, until all of the potato slices are used up.

5 Brush the top layer of potato slices with butter, cover the dish and cook in a preheated oven, 190°C/375°F/Gas Mark 5, for 1½ hours.

6 Turn out on to a warm ovenproof platter and return to the oven for a further 25–30 minutes until golden brown. Serve at once, garnished with herbs.

COOK'S TIP

Make sure that the potatoes are sliced very thinly until they are almost transparent, in order that they cook thoroughly.

COOK'S TIP

The butter holds the potato slices together so that the cooked dish can be turned out. Therefore, it is important that the potato slices are dried thoroughly with paper towels before layering them in the dish, otherwise the butter will not be able to stick to them.

Potatoes with Almonds & Cream

Serves 4

INGREDIENTS

2 large potatoes, unpeeled and sliced
1 tbsp vegetable oil
1 red onion, halved and sliced
50 g/1¾ oz almond flakes
½ tsp turmeric
300ml/½ pint/1¼ cups double (heavy) cream
1 garlic clove, crushed
125 g/4½ oz rocket (arugula)
salt and pepper

1 Cook the sliced potatoes in a saucepan of boiling water for 10 minutes. Drain thoroughly.

2 Heat the vegetable oil in a frying pan (skillet) and cook the onion and garlic for 3–4 minutes, stirring frequently.

3 Add the almonds, turmeric and potato slices to the frying pan (skillet) and cook for 2–3 minutes, stirring constantly. Stir in the rocket (arugula).

4 Transfer the potato and almond mixture to a shallow ovenproof dish. Pour the double (heavy) cream over the top and season with salt and pepper.

5 Cook in a preheated oven, 190°C/375°F/ Gas Mark 5, for 20 minutes or until the potatoes are cooked through. Serve as an accompaniment to grilled (broiled) meat or fish dishes.

VARIATION

You could use other nuts, such as unsalted peanuts or cashews, instead of the almond flakes, if you prefer.

VARIATION

If rocket (arugula) is unavailable, use the same quantity of trimmed baby spinach instead.

Casseroled Potatoes

Serves 4

INGREDIENTS

675 g/1½ lb waxy potatoes, cut into chunks
15 g/½ oz/1 tbsp butter
2 leeks, sliced
150 ml/¼ pint/⅔ cup dry white wine
150 ml/¼ pint/⅔ cup vegetable stock
1 tbsp lemon juice
2 tbsp chopped mixed fresh herbs
salt and pepper

TO GARNISH:
grated lemon rind
mixed fresh herbs (optional)

1 Cook the potato chunks in a saucepan of boiling water for 5 minutes. Drain thoroughly.

2 Meanwhile, melt the butter in a frying pan (skillet) and sauté the leeks for 5 minutes or until they have softened.

3 Spoon the partly cooked potatoes and leeks into the base of an ovenproof dish.

4 In a measuring jug, mix together the wine, vegetable stock, lemon juice and chopped mixed herbs. Season to taste with salt and pepper, then pour the mixture over the potatoes.

5 Cook in a preheated oven, 190°C/375°F/ Gas Mark 5, for 35 minutes or until the potatoes are tender.

6 Garnish the potato casserole with lemon rind and fresh herbs, if using, and serve as an accompaniment to meat casseroles or roast meat.

COOK'S TIP

Cover the ovenproof dish halfway through cooking if the leeks start to brown on the top.

Cheese Crumble-Topped Mash

Serves 4

INGREDIENTS

900 g/2 lb floury (mealy) potatoes, diced
25 g/1 oz/2 tbsp butter
2 tbsp milk
50 g/1¾ oz mature (sharp) cheese or blue cheese, grated

CRUMBLE TOPPING:
40 g/1½ oz/3 tbsp butter
1 onion, cut into chunks
1 garlic clove, crushed
1 tbsp wholegrain mustard
175 g/ 6 oz/3 cups fresh wholemeal (whole wheat) breadcrumbs
2 tbsp chopped fresh parsley
salt and pepper

1 Cook the potatoes in a pan of boiling water for 10 minutes or until cooked through.

2 Meanwhile, make the crumble topping. Melt the butter in a frying pan (skillet). Add the onion, garlic and mustard and fry gently for 5 minutes until the onion chunks have softened, stirring constantly.

3 Put the breadcrumbs in a mixing bowl and stir in the fried onion. Season to taste with salt and pepper.

4 Drain the potatoes thoroughly and place them in a mixing bowl. Add the butter and milk, then mash until smooth. Stir in the grated cheese while the potato is still hot.

5 Spoon the mashed potato into a shallow ovenproof dish and sprinkle with the crumble topping.

6 Cook in a preheated oven, 200°C/400°F/ Gas Mark 6, for 10–15 minutes until the crumble topping is golden brown and crunchy. Serve immediately.

COOK'S TIP

For extra crunch, add freshly cooked vegetables, such as celery and (bell) peppers, to the mashed potato in step 4.

Carrot & Potato Soufflé

Serves 4

INGREDIENTS

25 g/1 oz/2 tbsp butter, melted
4 tbsp fresh wholemeal (whole wheat) breadcrumbs
675 g/1½ lb floury (mealy) potatoes, baked in their skins
2 carrots, grated
2 eggs, separated
2 tbsp orange juice
¼ tsp grated nutmeg
salt and pepper
carrot curls, to garnish

1 Brush the inside of a 900 ml/1½ pint/3¾ cup soufflé dish with butter. Sprinkle three quarters of the breadcrumbs over the base and sides of the dish.

2 Cut the baked potatoes in half and scoop the flesh into a mixing bowl.

3 Add the carrot, egg yolks, orange juice and nutmeg to the potato flesh. Season to taste with salt and pepper.

4 In a separate bowl, whisk the egg whites until they stand in soft peaks, then gently fold into the potato mixture with a metal spoon until well incorporated.

5 Gently spoon the potato and carrot mixture into the prepared soufflé dish. Sprinkle the remaining breadcrumbs over the top of the mixture.

6 Cook in a preheated oven, 200°C/400°F/ Gas Mark 6, for 40 minutes until risen and golden. Do not open the oven door during the cooking time, otherwise the soufflé will sink. Serve at once, garnished with carrot curls.

COOK'S TIP

To bake the potatoes, prick the skins and cook in a preheated oven, 190°C/375°F/Gas Mark 5, for about 1 hour.

Steamed Potatoes En Papillotes

Serves 4

INGREDIENTS

16 small new potatoes
1 carrot, cut into matchstick strips
1 fennel bulb, sliced
75 g/2¾ oz French (green) beans
1 yellow (bell) pepper, cut into strips
16 tbsp dry white wine
4 rosemary sprigs
salt and pepper
rosemary sprigs, to garnish

1 Cut 4 squares of greaseproof (waxed) paper measuring about 25 cm/10 inches in size.

2 Divide the vegetables equally between the 4 paper squares, placing them in the centre.

3 Bring the edges of the paper together and scrunch them together to encase the vegetables, leaving the top open.

4 Place the parcels in a shallow roasting tin (pan) and spoon 4 tbsp of white wine into each parcel. Add a rosemary sprig and season with salt and pepper

5 Fold the top of each parcel over to seal it. Cook in a preheated oven, 190°C/375°F/Gas Mark 5, for 30–35 minutes or until the vegetables are tender.

6 Transfer the sealed parcels to 4 individual serving plates and garnish with rosemary sprigs. The parcels should be opened at the table in order for the full aroma of the vegetables to be appreciated.

COOK'S TIP

These parcels may be cooked in a steamer, if preferred.

VARIATION

If small new potatoes are unavailable, use larger potatoes which have been halved or quartered to ensure that they cook through in the specified cooking time.

Main Meals

This chapter contains a wide selection of delicious main meal dishes which are more substantial than the snacks and light meal section and generally require more preparation and cooking. The potato is the main ingredient in the majority of the recipes in this chapter, but they also include ideas for adding meat, poultry, fish and vegetarian ingredients – so that there is sure to be something for everyone.

The recipes come from all around the world – try Potato Ravioli, Potato & Lamb Kofta, Spanish Potato Bake or Potato Curry. There are also lots of hearty and filling dishes, including Creamy Chicken & Potato Casserole, Four Cheese & Potato Layer Bake and Potato & Aubergine (Eggplant) Gratin. Whether you are cooking for one or two, a family or a number of guests at a dinner party, you will find something here to entice you!

Potato, Beef & Peanut Pot

Serves 4

INGREDIENTS

1 tbsp vegetable oil
60 g/2 oz/¼ cup butter
450 g/1 lb lean beef steak, cut into thin strips
1 onion, halved and sliced
2 garlic cloves, crushed
2 large waxy potatoes, cubed
½ tsp paprika
4 tbsp crunchy peanut butter
600 ml/1 pint/2½ cups beef stock
25 g/1 oz unsalted peanuts
2 tsp light soy sauce
50 g/1¾ oz sugar snap peas
1 red (bell) pepper, cut into strips
parsley sprigs, to garnish (optional)

1 Heat the oil and butter in a flameproof casserole dish.

2 Add the beef strips and fry them gently for 3–4 minutes, stirring and turning the meat until it is sealed on all sides.

3 Add the onion and garlic and cook for a further 2 minutes, stirring constantly.

4 Add the potato cubes and cook for 3–4 minutes or until they begin to brown slightly.

5 Stir in the paprika and peanut butter, then gradually blend in the beef stock. Bring the mixture to the boil, stirring frequently.

6 Finally, add the peanuts, soy sauce, sugar snap peas and red (bell) pepper.

7 Cover and cook over a low heat for 45 minutes or until the beef is cooked through.

8 Garnish the dish with parsley sprigs, if wished, and serve.

COOK'S TIP

Serve this dish with plain boiled rice or noodles, if you wish.

VARIATION

Add a chopped green chilli to the sauce for extra spice, if you prefer.

Potato Ravioli

Serves 4

INGREDIENTS

FILLING:
1 tbsp vegetable oil
125 g/4½ oz ground beef
1 shallot, diced
1 garlic clove, crushed
1 tbsp plain (all-purpose) flour
1 tbsp tomato purée (paste)
150 ml/¼ pint/⅔ cup beef stock
1 celery stick, chopped
2 tomatoes, peeled and diced
2 tsp chopped fresh basil
salt and pepper

RAVIOLI:
450 g/1 lb floury (mealy) potatoes, diced
3 small egg yolks
3 tbsp olive oil
175 g/6 oz/1½ cups plain (all-purpose) flour
60 g/2 oz/¼ cup butter, for frying
shredded basil leaves, to garnish

1 To make the filling, heat the oil in a pan and fry the beef for 3–4 minutes, breaking it up with a spoon. Add the shallot and garlic and cook for 2–3 minutes until the shallot has softened.

2 Stir in the flour and tomato purée (paste) and cook for 1 minute. Stir in the beef stock, celery, tomatoes and chopped fresh basil. Season to taste with salt and pepper.

3 Cook the mixture over a low heat for 20 minutes. Remove from the heat and leave to cool.

4 To make the ravioli, cook the potatoes in a pan of boiling water for 10 minutes until cooked.

5 Mash the potatoes and place them in a mixing bowl. Blend in the egg yolks and oil. Season with salt and pepper, then stir in the flour and mix to form a dough.

6 On a lightly floured surface, divide the dough into 24 pieces and shape into flat rounds. Spoon the filling on to one half of each round and fold the dough over to encase the filling, pressing down to seal the edges.

7 Melt the butter in a frying pan (skillet) and cook the ravioli for 6–8 minutes, turning once, until golden. Serve hot, garnished with shredded basil leaves.

6

6

7

Veal Italienne

Serves 4

INGREDIENTS

60 g/2 oz/¼ cup butter
1 tbsp olive oil
675 g/1½ lb potatoes, cubed
4 veal escalopes, weighing about 175 g/6 oz each
1 onion, cut into 8 wedges
2 garlic cloves, crushed
2 tbsp plain (all-purpose) flour
2 tbsp tomato purée (paste)
150 ml/¼ pint/⅔ cup red wine
300 ml/½ pint/1¼ cups chicken stock
8 ripe tomatoes, peeled, seeded and diced
25 g/1 oz stoned (pitted) black olives, halved
2 tbsp chopped fresh basil
salt and pepper
fresh basil leaves, to garnish

1 Heat the butter and oil in a large frying pan (skillet). Add the potato cubes and cook for 5–7 minutes, stirring frequently, until they begin to brown.

2 Remove the potatoes from the pan (skillet) with a perforated spoon and set aside.

3 Place the veal in the frying pan (skillet) and cook for 2-3 minutes on each side until sealed. Remove from the pan and set aside.

4 Stir the onion and garlic into the pan (skillet) and cook for 2–3 minutes.

5 Add the flour and tomato purée (paste) and cook for 1 minute, stirring. Gradually blend in the red wine and chicken stock, stirring to make a smooth sauce.

6 Return the potatoes and veal to the pan (skillet). Stir in the tomatoes, olives and chopped basil and season with salt and pepper.

7 Transfer to a casserole dish and cook in a preheated oven, 180°C/350°F/Gas Mark 4, for 1 hour or until the potatoes and veal are cooked through. Garnish with basil leaves and serve.

COOK'S TIP

For a quicker cooking time and really tender meat, pound the meat with a meat mallet to flatten it slightly before cooking.

Lamb Hotpot

Serves 4

INGREDIENTS

675 g/1$\frac{1}{2}$ lb best end of lamb neck cutlets
2 lamb's kidneys
1 large onion, sliced thinly
675 g/1$\frac{1}{2}$ lb waxy potatoes, scrubbed and sliced thinly
2 tbsp chopped fresh thyme
150 ml/$\frac{1}{4}$ pint/$\frac{2}{3}$ cup lamb stock
25 g/1 oz/2 tbsp butter, melted
salt and pepper
fresh thyme sprigs, to garnish

1 Remove any excess fat from the lamb. Skin and core the kidneys and cut them into slices.

2 Arrange a layer of potatoes in the base of a 1.8 litre/3 pint/3$\frac{1}{2}$ cup ovenproof dish.

3 Arrange the lamb neck cutlets on top of the potatoes and cover with the sliced kidneys, onion and chopped fresh thyme.

4 Pour the lamb stock over the meat and season to taste with salt and pepper.

5 Layer the remaining potato slices on top, overlapping to completely cover the meat and sliced onion.

6 Brush the potato slices with the butter, cover the dish and cook in a preheated oven, 180°C/ 350°F/ Gas Mark 4, for 1$\frac{1}{2}$ hours.

7 Remove the lid and cook for a further 30 minutes until golden brown on top.

8 Garnish with fresh thyme sprigs and serve hot.

COOK'S TIP

Although this is a classic recipe, extra ingredients of your choice, such as celery or carrots, can be added to the dish for variety and colour.

VARIATION

Traditionally, oysters are also included in this tasty hotpot. Add them to the layers along with the kidneys, if wished.

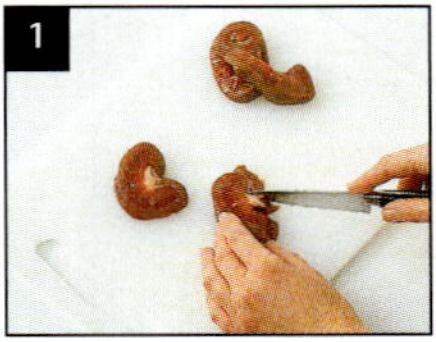

Potato & Lamb Kofta

Serves 4

INGREDIENTS

450 g/1 lb floury (mealy) potatoes, diced
25 g/1 oz/2 tbsp butter
225 g/8 oz minced lamb
1 onion, chopped
2 garlic cloves, crushed
½ tsp ground coriander
2 eggs, beaten
oil, for deep-frying
mint sprigs, to garnish

SAUCE:
150 ml/¼ pint/⅔ cup natural yogurt
50 g/2 oz cucumber, finely chopped
1 tbsp chopped mint
1 garlic clove, crushed

1 Cook the diced potatoes in a saucepan of boiling water for 10 minutes until cooked through. Drain, mash until smooth and transfer to a mixing bowl.

2 Melt the butter in a frying pan (skillet), add the lamb, onion, garlic and coriander and fry for 15 minutes, stirring.

3 Drain off the liquid from the pan, then stir the meat mixture into the mashed potatoes. Stir in the eggs and season.

4 To make the sauce, combine the yogurt, cucumber, mint and garlic in a bowl and set aside.

5 Heat the oil in a large saucepan or a deep fat fryer to 180°C–190°C/350°F–375°F, or until a cube of bread browns in 30 seconds. Drop spoonfuls of the potato mixture into the hot oil and cook in batches for 4–5 minutes or until golden brown.

6 Remove the kofta with a perforated spoon, drain thoroughly on paper towels, set aside and keep warm. Garnish with fresh mint sprigs and serve with the sauce.

COOK'S TIP

These kofta can be made with any sort of minced meat, such as turkey, chicken or pork, and flavoured with appropriate fresh herbs, such as sage or coriander (cilantro).

Spanish Potato Bake

Serves 4

INGREDIENTS

675 g/1½ lb waxy potatoes, diced
3 tbsp olive oil
1 onion, halved and sliced
2 garlic cloves, crushed
400 g/14 oz can plum tomatoes, chopped
75 g/2¾ oz chorizo sausage, sliced
1 green (bell) pepper, cut into strips
½ tsp paprika
25 g/1 oz stoned (pitted) black olives, halved
8 eggs
1 tbsp chopped fresh parsley
salt and pepper

1 Cook the diced potatoes in a saucepan of boiling water for 10 minutes or until softened. Drain and set aside.

2 Heat the olive oil in a large frying pan (skillet), add the sliced onion and garlic and fry gently for 2–3 minutes until the onion softens.

3 Add the chopped canned tomatoes and cook over a low heat for about 10 minutes until the mixture has reduced slightly.

4 Stir the potatoes into the pan with the chorizo, green (bell) pepper, paprika and olives. Cook for 5 minutes, stirring. Transfer to a shallow ovenproof dish.

5 Make 8 small hollows in the top of the mixture and break an egg into each hollow.

6 Cook in a preheated oven, 225°C/425°F/ Gas Mark 7, for 5–6 minutes or until the eggs are just cooked. Sprinkle with parsley and serve with crusty bread.

VARIATION

Add a little spice to the dish by incorporating 1 tsp chilli powder in step 4, if wished.

Potato & Pepperoni Pizza

Makes 1 large pizza

INGREDIENTS

900 g/2 lb floury (mealy) potatoes, diced
15 g/½ oz/1 tbsp butter
2 garlic cloves, crushed
2 tbsp mixed chopped fresh herbs
1 egg, beaten
85 ml/3 fl oz/⅓ cup passata
2 tbsp tomato purée (paste)
50 g/1¾ oz pepperoni slices
1 green (bell) pepper, cut into strips
1 yellow (bell) pepper, cut into strips
2 large open cap mushrooms, sliced
25 g/1 oz stoned (pitted) black olives, quartered
125 g/4½ oz Mozzarella cheese, sliced

1 Grease and flour a 23 cm/9 inch pizza tin (pan).

2 Cook the diced potatoes in a saucepan of boiling water for 10 minutes or until cooked through. Drain and mash until smooth. Transfer the mashed potato to a mixing bowl and stir in the butter, garlic, herbs and egg.

3 Spread the mixture into the prepared pizza pan. Cook in a preheated oven, 225°C/425°F/Gas Mark 7, for 7–10 minutes or until the pizza base begins to set.

4 Mix the passata and tomato purée (paste) together and spoon it over the pizza base, to within 1 cm/½ inch of the edge of the base.

5 Arrange the pepperoni, (bell) peppers, mushrooms and olives on top of the passata.

6 Scatter the Mozzarella cheese on top of the pizza. Cook in the oven for 20 minutes or until the base is cooked through and the cheese has melted on top. Serve hot with a mixed salad.

COOK'S TIP

This pizza base is softer in texture than a normal bread dough and is ideal served from the tin (pan). Top with any of your favourite pizza ingredients that you have to hand.

Potato & Sausage Panfry

Serves 4

INGREDIENTS

675 g/$1\frac{1}{2}$ lb waxy potatoes, cubed
25 g/1 oz/2 tbsp butter
8 large herb sausages
4 smoked bacon slices
1 onion, quartered
1 courgette (zucchini), sliced
150 ml/$\frac{1}{4}$ pint/$\frac{2}{3}$ cup dry white wine
300 ml/$\frac{1}{2}$ pint/$1\frac{1}{4}$ cups vegetable stock
1 tsp Worcestershire sauce
2 tbsp chopped mixed fresh herbs
salt and pepper
chopped fresh herbs, to garnish

1 Cook the cubed potatoes in a saucepan of boiling water for 10 minutes or until softened. Drain thoroughly and set aside.

2 Meanwhile, melt the butter in a large frying pan (skillet). Add the herb sausages and cook for 5 minutes, turning them frequently to ensure that they brown on all sides.

3 Add the bacon slices, onion, courgette (zucchini) and potatoes to the pan. Cook the mixture for a further 10 minutes, stirring the mixture and turning the sausages frequently.

4 Stir in the white wine, stock, Worcestershire sauce and chopped mixed herbs. Season with salt and pepper to taste and cook the mixture over a gentle heat for 10 minutes. Season with a little more salt and pepper, if necessary.

5 Transfer the potato and sausage panfry to warm serving plates, garnish with chopped fresh herbs and serve at once.

COOK'S TIP

Use different flavours of sausage to vary the dish – there are many different varieties available, such as leek and mustard.

VARIATION

For an attractive colour, use a red onion cut into quarters rather than a white onion.

2

3

4

Potato, Tomato & Sausage Panfry

Serves 4

INGREDIENTS

2 large potatoes, sliced
1 tbsp vegetable oil
8 flavoured sausages
1 red onion, cut into 8
1 tbsp tomato purée (paste)
150 ml/¼ pint/⅔ cup red wine
150 ml/¼ pint/⅔ cup passata
2 large tomatoes, each cut into 8
175 g/6 oz broccoli florets, blanched
2 tbsp chopped fresh basil
salt and pepper
shredded fresh basil, to garnish

1 Cook the sliced potatoes in a saucepan of boiling water for 7 minutes. Drain thoroughly and set aside.

2 Meanwhile, heat the oil in a large frying pan (skillet). Add the sausages and cook for 5 minutes, turning the sausages frequently to ensure that they are browned on all sides.

3 Add the onion pieces to the pan and continue to cook for a further 5 minutes, stirring the mixture frequently.

4 Stir in the tomato purée (paste), red wine and the passata and mix together well. Add the tomato wedges, broccoli florets and chopped basil to the panfry and mix carefully.

5 Add the parboiled potato slices to the pan. Cook the mixture for about 10 minutes or until the sausages are completely cooked through. Season to taste with salt and pepper.

6 Garnish the panfry with fresh shredded basil and serve hot.

COOK'S TIP

Omit the passata from this recipe and use canned plum tomatoes or chopped tomatoes for convenience.

VARIATION

Broccoli is particularly good in this dish as it adds a splash of colour, but other vegetables of your choice can be used instead, if preferred.

3

4

5

Potato, Chicken & Banana Cakes

Serves 4

INGREDIENTS

450 g/1 lb floury (mealy) potatoes, diced
225 g/8 oz minced chicken
1 large banana
2 tbsp plain (all purpose) flour
1 tsp lemon juice
1 onion, finely chopped
2 tbsp chopped fresh sage
25 g/1 oz/2 tbsp butter
2 tbsp vegetable oil
150 ml/¼ pint/⅔ cup single (light) cream
150 ml/¼ pint/⅔ cup chicken stock
salt and pepper
fresh sage leaves, to garnish

1 Cook the diced potatoes in a saucepan of boiling water for 10 minutes until cooked through. Drain and mash the potatoes until smooth. Stir in the chicken.

2 Mash the banana and add it to the potato with the flour, lemon juice, onion and half of the chopped sage. Season well and stir the mixture together.

3 Divide the mixture into 8 equal portions. With lightly floured hands, shape each portion into a round patty.

4 Heat the butter and oil in a frying pan (skillet), add the potato cakes and cook for 12–15 minutes or until cooked through, turning once. Remove from the pan (skillet) and keep warm.

5 Stir the cream and stock into the pan (skillet) with the remaining chopped sage. Cook over a low heat for 2–3 minutes.

6 Arrange the potato cakes on a serving plate, garnish with fresh sage leaves and serve with the cream and sage sauce.

COOK'S TIP

Do not boil the sauce once the cream has been added as it will curdle. Cook it gently over a very low heat.

Creamy Chicken & Potato Casserole

Serves 4

INGREDIENTS

2 tbsp vegetable oil
60 g/2 oz/¼ cup butter
4 chicken portions, about 225 g/8 oz each
2 leeks, sliced
1 garlic clove, crushed
4 tbsp plain (all-purpose) flour
900 ml/1½ pints/3¾ cups chicken stock
300 ml/½ pint/1¼ cups dry white wine
125 g/4½ oz baby carrots, halved lengthways
125 g/4½ oz baby sweetcorn cobs (baby corn), halved lengthways
450 g/1 lb small new potatoes
1 bouquet garni
150 ml/¼ pint/⅔ cup double (heavy) cream
salt and pepper

1 Heat the oil in a large frying pan (skillet). Cook the chicken for 10 minutes, turning until browned all over. Transfer the chicken to a casserole dish using a perforated spoon.

2 Add the leek and garlic to the frying pan (skillet) and cook for 2–3 minutes, stirring. Stir in the flour and cook for a further 1 minute. Remove the frying pan (skillet) from the heat and stir in the stock and wine. Season well.

3 Return the pan to the heat and bring the mixture to the boil. Stir in the carrots, sweetcorn, potatoes and bouquet garni.

4 Transfer the mixture to the casserole dish. Cover and cook in a preheated oven, 180°C/350°F/Gas Mark 4, for about 1 hour.

5 Remove the casserole from the oven and stir in the cream. Return the casserole to the oven, uncovered, and cook for a further 15 minutes.

Remove the bouquet garni and discard. Taste and adjust the seasoning, if necessary. Serve the casserole with plain rice or fresh vegetables, such as broccoli.

COOK'S TIP

Use turkey fillets instead of the chicken, if preferred, and vary the vegetables according to those you have to hand.

1

3

5

Potato-Topped Cod

Serves 4

INGREDIENTS

60 g/2 oz/¼ cup butter
4 waxy potatoes, sliced
1 large onion, finely chopped
1 tsp wholegrain mustard
1 tsp garam masala
pinch of chilli powder
1 tbsp chopped fresh dill
75 g/2¾ oz/1¼ cups fresh breadcrumbs
4 cod fillets, about 175 g/6 oz each
50 g/1¾ oz Gruyère cheese, grated
salt and pepper
fresh dill sprigs, to garnish

1 Melt half of the butter in a frying pan (skillet). Add the potatoes and fry for 5 minutes, turning until they are browned all over. Remove the potatoes from the pan with a perforated spoon.

2 Add the remaining butter to the frying pan (skillet) and stir in the onion, mustard, garam masala, chilli powder, chopped dill and breadcrumbs. Cook for 1–2 minutes, stirring and mixing well.

3 Layer half of the potatoes in the base of an ovenproof dish and place the cod fillets on top. Cover the cod fillets with the rest of the potato slices. Season to taste with salt and pepper.

4 Spoon the spicy mixture from the frying pan (skillet) over the potato and sprinkle with the grated cheese.

5 Cook in a preheated oven, 200°C/400°F/ Gas Mark 6, for 20–25 minutes or until the topping is golden and crisp and the fish is cooked through. Garnish with fresh dill sprigs and serve at once.

COOK'S TIP

This dish is ideal served with baked vegetables which can be cooked in the oven at the same time.

VARIATION

You can use any fish for this recipe: for special occasions use salmon steaks or fillets.

Potato Curry

Serves 4

INGREDIENTS

4 tbsp vegetable oil
675 g/1½ lb waxy potatoes, cut into large chunks
2 onions, quartered
3 garlic cloves, crushed
1 tsp garam masala
½ tsp turmeric
½ tsp ground cumin
½ tsp ground coriander
2.5 cm/1 inch piece ginger root, grated
1 red chilli, chopped
225 g/8 oz cauliflower florets
4 tomatoes, peeled and quartered
75 g/2¾ oz frozen peas
2 tbsp chopped fresh coriander (cilantro)
300 ml/½ pint/1¼ cups vegetable stock
shredded fresh coriander (cilantro), to garnish

1 Heat the vegetable oil in a large heavy-based saucepan or frying pan (skillet). Add the potato chunks, onion and garlic and fry gently for 2–3 minutes, stirring the mixture frequently.

2 Add the garam masala, turmeric, ground cumin, ground coriander, grated ginger and chopped chilli to the pan, mixing the spices into the vegetables. Fry for 1 minute, stirring constantly.

3 Add the cauliflower florets, tomatoes, peas, chopped coriander (cilantro) and vegetable stock to the curry mixture.

4 Cook the potato curry over a low heat for 30–40 minutes or until the potatoes are completely cooked through.

5 Garnish the potato curry with fresh coriander (cilantro) and serve with plain boiled rice or warm Indian bread.

COOK'S TIP

Use a large heavy-based saucepan or frying pan (skillet) for this recipe to ensure that the potatoes are cooked thoroughly.

Potato & Spinach Gnocchi

Serves 4

INGREDIENTS

300 g/10½ oz floury (mealy) potatoes, diced
175 g/6 oz spinach
125 g/4½ oz/1 cup plain (all-purpose) flour
1 egg yolk
1 tsp olive oil
salt and pepper
spinach leaves, to garnish

SAUCE:
1 tbsp olive oil
2 shallots, chopped
1 garlic clove, crushed
300 ml/½ pint/1¼ cups passata
2 tsp soft light brown sugar

1 Cook the diced potatoes in a saucepan of boiling water for 10 minutes until cooked through. Drain and mash the potatoes.

2 Meanwhile, in a separate pan, blanch the spinach in a little boiling water for 1–2 minutes. Drain well and shred the leaves.

3 Transfer the mashed potato to a lightly floured chopping board and make a well in the centre. Add the egg yolk, olive oil, spinach and a little of the flour and quickly mix the ingredients into the potato, adding more flour as you go, until you have a firm dough. Divide the mixture into very small dumplings.

4 Cook the gnocchi in batches in a saucepan of boiling salted water for about 5 minutes or until they rise to the top of the pan.

5 Meanwhile, make the sauce. Put the oil, shallots, garlic, passata and sugar into a saucepan and cook over a low heat for 10–15 minutes or until the sauce has thickened.

6 Drain the gnocchi using a perforated spoon and transfer to warm serving dishes. Spoon the sauce over the gnocchi and garnish with the fresh spinach leaves.

VARIATION

Add chopped fresh herbs and cheese to the gnocchi dough instead of the spinach, if you prefer.

Potato-Topped Vegetables in Wine

Serves 4

INGREDIENTS

1 carrot, diced
175 g/6 oz cauliflower florets
175 g/6 oz broccoli florets
1 fennel bulb, sliced
75 g/2$^{3}/_{4}$ oz green beans, halved
25 g/1 oz/2 tbsp butter
25 g/1 oz/$^{1}/_{4}$ cup plain (all-purpose) flour
150 ml/$^{1}/_{4}$ pint/$^{2}/_{3}$ cup vegetable stock
150 ml/$^{1}/_{4}$ pint/$^{2}/_{3}$ cup dry white wine
150 ml/$^{1}/_{4}$ pint/$^{2}/_{3}$ cup milk
2 tbsp chopped fresh sage
175 g/6 oz chestnut mushrooms, quartered

TOPPING:
4 floury (mealy) potatoes, diced
25 g/1 oz/2 tbsp butter
4 tbsp natural yogurt
4 tbsp grated Parmesan cheese
1 tsp fennel seeds
salt and pepper

1 Cook the carrot, cauliflower, broccoli, fennel and beans in a saucepan of boiling water for 10 minutes. Drain the vegetables thoroughly and set aside.

2 Melt the butter in a saucepan and stir in the flour. Cook for 1 minute, then remove from the heat. Stir in the stock, wine and milk and bring to the boil, stirring until thickened. Stir in the reserved vegetables and mushrooms.

3 Meanwhile, make the topping. Cook the diced potatoes in a separate pan of boiling water for 10–15 minutes or until cooked through. Drain the potatoes and mash with the butter, yogurt and half of the cheese. Stir in the fennel seeds.

4 Spoon the vegetable mixture into a 1 litre/ 1$^{3}/_{4}$ pint /4 cup pie dish. Spoon or pipe the potato over the top, covering the filling completely. Sprinkle the remaining cheese on top. Cook in a preheated oven, 190°C/375°F/Gas Mark 5, for 30–35 minutes or until the topping is golden. Serve hot.

COOK'S TIP

Any combination of vegetables may be used in this dish, and frozen mixed vegetables can be defrosted and used for convenience and speed.

1

2

4

Potato & Three Cheese Soufflé

Serves 4

INGREDIENTS

25 g/1 oz/2 tbsp butter
2 tsp plain (all-purpose) flour
900 g/2 lb floury (mealy) potatoes
8 eggs, separated
25 g/1 oz Gruyère cheese, grated
25 g/1 oz mature (sharp) cheese, grated
25 g/1 oz blue cheese, crumbled
salt and pepper

1 Butter a 2.4 litre/4 pint/10 cup soufflé dish and dust with the flour. Set aside.

2 Cook the potatoes in a saucepan of boiling water until cooked through. Mash until very smooth and transfer to a mixing bowl to cool.

3 Whisk the egg yolks into the potato and stir in the 3 different cheeses. Season well with salt and pepper.

4 In a clean bowl, whisk the egg whites until standing in peaks, then gently fold them into the potato mixture with a metal spoon until fully incorporated.

5 Spoon the potato mixture into the prepared soufflé dish.

6 Cook in a preheated oven, 220°C/425°F/Gas Mark 7, for 35–40 minutes until risen and set. Serve immediately.

COOK'S TIP

Insert a fine skewer into the centre of the soufflé; it should come out clean when the soufflé is fully cooked through.

VARIATION

You can add chopped cooked bacon to the soufflé for extra flavour, if wished.

Nutty Harvest Loaf

Serves 4

INGREDIENTS

450 g/1 lb floury (mealy) potatoes, diced
25 g/1 oz/2 tbsp butter
1 onion, chopped
2 garlic cloves, crushed
125 g/4½ oz unsalted peanuts
75 g/2¾ oz fresh white breadcrumbs
1 egg, beaten
2 tbsp chopped fresh coriander (cilantro)
150 ml/¼ pint/⅔ cup vegetable stock
75 g/2¾ oz closed cap mushrooms, sliced
50 g/1¾ oz sun-dried tomatoes, sliced
salt and pepper

SAUCE:
150 ml/¼ pint/⅔ cup crème fraîche
2 tsp tomato purée (paste)
2 tsp clear honey
2 tbsp chopped fresh coriander (cilantro)

1 Grease a 450 g/1 lb loaf tin (pan). Cook the potatoes in a saucepan of boiling water for 10 minutes until cooked through. Drain well, mash and set aside.

2 Melt half of the butter in a frying pan (skillet). Add the onion and garlic and fry gently for 2–3 minutes until soft. Finely chop the nuts or blend them in a food processor for 30 seconds with the breadcrumbs.

3 Mix the chopped nuts and breadcrumbs into the potatoes with the egg, coriander (cilantro) and vegetable stock. Stir in the onion and garlic and mix well.

4 Melt the remaining butter in the frying pan (skillet), add the sliced mushrooms and cook for 2–3 minutes.

5 Press half of the potato mixture into the base of the loaf tin (pan). Spoon the mushrooms on top and sprinkle with the sun-dried tomatoes. Spoon the remaining potato mixture on top and smooth the surface. Cover with foil and bake in a preheated oven, 190°C/ 350°F/ Gas Mark 5, for 1 hour or until firm to the touch.

6 Meanwhile, mix the sauce ingredients together. Cut the nutty harvest loaf into slices and serve with the sauce.

3

5

5

Vegetable Cake

Serves 4

INGREDIENTS

BASE:
2 tbsp vegetable oil
4 large waxy potatoes, sliced thinly

TOPPING:
1 tbsp vegetable oil
1 leek, chopped
1 courgette (zucchini), grated
1 red (bell) pepper, diced
1 green (bell) pepper, diced
1 carrot, grated
2 tsp chopped fresh parsley
225 g/8 oz full fat soft cheese
25 g/1 oz mature (sharp) cheese, grated
2 eggs, beaten
salt and pepper
shredded cooked leek, to garnish

1 Grease a 20 cm/8 inch springform cake tin (pan).

2 To make the base, heat the oil in a frying pan (skillet). Cook the potato slices in batches over a medium heat until softened and browned. Drain thoroughly on paper towels and arrange the slices in the base of the tin (pan).

3 To make the topping, heat the oil in a separate frying pan (skillet) and fry the leek over a low heat for 3–4 minutes until softened.

4 Add the courgette (zucchini), (bell) peppers, carrot and parsley to the pan and cook over a low heat for 5–7 minutes or until the vegetables have softened.

5 Meanwhile, beat the cheeses and eggs together in a bowl. Stir in the vegetables and season to taste with salt and pepper. Spoon the mixture on to the potato base.

6 Cook in a preheated oven, 190°C/375°F/ Gas Mark 5, for 20–25 minutes until the cake is set.

7 Remove the vegetable cake from the tin (pan), garnish with shredded leek and serve with a crisp salad.

COOK'S TIP

Add diced tofu (bean curd) or diced meat, such as pork or chicken, to the topping, if wished. Cook the meat with the vegetables in step 4.

Bubble & Squeak

Serves 4

INGREDIENTS

450 g/1 lb floury (mealy) potatoes, diced
225 g/8 oz Savoy cabbage, shredded
5 tbsp vegetable oil
2 leeks, chopped
1 garlic clove, crushed
225 g/8 oz smoked tofu (bean curd), cubed
salt and pepper
shredded cooked leek, to garnish

1 Cook the diced potatoes in a saucepan of boiling water for 10 minutes until tender. Drain and mash the potatoes.

2 Meanwhile, in a separate saucepan blanch the cabbage in boiling water for 5 minutes. Drain and add to the potato.

3 Heat the oil in a heavy-based frying pan (skillet), add the leeks and garlic and fry gently for 2–3 minutes. Stir into the potato and cabbage mixture.

4 Add the smoked tofu (bean curd) and season well with salt and pepper. Cook over a moderate heat for 10 minutes.

5 Carefully turn the whole mixture over and continue to cook over a moderate heat for a further 5–7 minutes until crispy underneath. Serve immediately, garnished with shredded leek.

VARIATION

You can add cooked meats, such as beef or chicken, instead of the tofu (bean curd) for a more traditional recipe. Any gravy from the cooked meats can also be added, but ensure that the mixture is not too wet.

COOK'S TIP

This vegetarian recipe is a perfect main meal, as the smoked tofu (bean curd) cubes added to the basic bubble and squeak mixture make it very substantial.

Potato Hash

Serves 4

INGREDIENTS

25 g/1 oz/2 tbsp butter
1 red onion, halved and sliced
1 carrot, diced
25 g/1 oz French (green) beans, halved
3 large waxy potatoes, diced
2 tbsp plain (all purpose) flour
600 ml/1 pint/1¼ cups vegetable stock
225 g/8 oz tofu (bean curd), diced
salt and pepper
chopped fresh parsley, to garnish

1 Melt the butter in a frying pan (skillet). Add the onion, carrot, French (green) beans and potatoes and fry gently, stirring, for 5–7 minutes or until the vegetables begin to brown.

2 Add the flour to the frying pan (skillet) and cook for 1 minute, stirring constantly. Gradually pour in the stock.

3 Reduce the heat and leave the mixture to simmer for 15 minutes or until the potatoes are tender.

4 Add the diced tofu (bean curd) to the mixture and cook for a further 5 minutes. Season to taste with salt and pepper.

5 Sprinkle the chopped parsley over the top of the potato hash to garnish, then serve hot straight from the pan (skillet).

VARIATION

Use cooked diced meat, such as beef or lamb, instead of the tofu (bean curd) for a non-vegetarian dish.

COOK'S TIP

Hash is an American term meaning to chop food into small pieces. Therefore a traditional hash dish is made from chopped fresh ingredients, such as roast beef or corned beef, (bell) peppers, onion and celery, often served with gravy.

Twice Baked Potatoes with Pesto

Serves 4

INGREDIENTS

4 baking potatoes, about 225 g/8 oz each
150 ml/¼ pint/⅔ cup double (heavy) cream
1 tbsp lemon juice
2 garlic cloves, crushed
85 ml/3 fl oz/⅓ cup vegetable stock
3 tbsp chopped fresh basil
2 tbsp pine kernels (nuts)
2 tbsp grated Parmesan cheese
salt and pepper

1 Scrub the potatoes and prick the skins with a fork. Rub a little salt into the skins and place on a baking (cookie) sheet.

2 Cook in a preheated oven, 190°C/375°F/Gas Mark 5, for 1 hour or until the potatoes are cooked through and the skins crisp.

3 Remove the potatoes from the oven and cut them in half lengthways. Using a spoon, scoop the potato flesh into a mixing bowl, leaving a thin shell of potato inside the skins. Mash the potato flesh with a fork.

4 Meanwhile, mix the cream and stock in a saucepan and simmer for 8–10 minutes or until reduced by half.

5 Stir in the lemon juice, garlic and chopped basil and season to taste with salt and pepper. Stir the mixture into the potato flesh with the pine kernels (nuts).

6 Spoon the mixture back into the potato shells and sprinkle the Parmesan cheese on top. Return the potatoes to the oven for 10 minutes or until the cheese has browned. Serve with fresh salad.

VARIATION

Add full fat soft cheese or thinly sliced mushrooms to the mashed potato flesh in step 5, if you prefer.

3

4

6

Baked Potatoes with Guacamole & Salsa

Serves 4

INGREDIENTS

4 baking potatoes, about 225 g/ 8 oz each
1 large ripe avocado
175 g/6 oz smoked tofu (bean curd), diced
2 garlic cloves, crushed
1 onion, chopped finely
1 tomato, chopped finely
1 tsp lemon juice
125 g/4½ oz mixed salad leaves
fresh coriander (cilantro) sprigs, to garnish

SALSA:
2 ripe tomatoes, seeded and diced
1 tbsp chopped coriander (cilantro)
1 shallot, diced finely
1 green chilli, diced
1 tbsp lemon juice
salt and pepper

1 Scrub the potatoes and prick the skins with a fork. Rub a little salt into the skins and place them on a baking (cookie) sheet.

2 Cook in a preheated oven, 190°C/375°F/ Gas Mark 5, for 1 hour or until cooked through and the skins are crisp.

3 Cut the potatoes in half lengthways and scoop the flesh into a bowl, leaving a thin layer of potato inside the shells.

4 Halve and stone the avocado. Using a spoon, scoop out the avocado flesh and add to the bowl containing the potato. Stir in the lemon juice and mash the mixture together with a fork. Mix in the tofu (bean curd), garlic, onion and tomato. Spoon the mixture into one half of the potato shells.

5 Arrange the salad leaves on top of the guacamole mixture and place the other half of the potato shell on top.

6 To make the salsa, mix the tomatoes, coriander (cilantro), shallots, chilli, lemon juice and salt and pepper to taste in a bowl. Garnish the potatoes with sprigs of fresh coriander (cilantro) and serve with the salsa.

Pan Potato Cake

Serves 4

INGREDIENTS

675 g/1½ lb waxy potatoes, unpeeled and sliced
1 carrot, diced
225 g/8 oz small broccoli florets
60 g/2 oz/¼ cup butter
2 tbsp vegetable oil
1 red onion, quartered
2 garlic cloves, crushed
175 g/6 oz tofu (bean curd), diced
2 tbsp chopped fresh sage
75 g/2¾ oz mature (sharp) cheese, grated

1 Cook the sliced potatoes in a saucepan of boiling water for 10 minutes. Drain thoroughly.

2 Meanwhile, cook the carrot and broccoli in a separate pan of boiling water for 5 minutes. Drain with a perforated spoon.

3 Heat the butter and oil in a 23 cm/9 inch frying pan (skillet), add the onion and garlic and fry gently for 2–3 minutes. Add half of the potatoes slices to the frying pan (skillet), covering the base of the pan (skillet).

4 Cover the potato slices with the carrot, broccoli and the tofu (bean curd). Sprinkle with half of the sage and cover with the remaining potato slices. Sprinkle the grated cheese over the top.

5 Cook over a moderate heat for 8–10 minutes, then heat under a preheated medium grill (broiler) for 2–3 minutes or until the cheese melts and browns.

6 Garnish with the remaining sage and serve straight from the pan (skillet).

COOK'S TIP

Make sure that the mixture fills the whole width of your frying pan (skillet) to enable the layers to remain intact.

Four Cheese & Potato Layer Bake

Serves 4

INGREDIENTS

900 g/2 lb unpeeled waxy potatoes, cut into wedges
25 g/1 oz/2 tbsp butter
1 red onion, halved and sliced
2 garlic cloves, crushed
25 g/1 oz/¼ cup plain (all purpose) flour
600 ml/1 pint/2½ cups milk
397 g/14 oz can artichoke hearts in brine, drained and halved
150 g/5½ oz frozen mixed vegetables, thawed
125 g/4½ oz Gruyère cheese, grated
125 g/4½ oz mature (sharp) cheese, grated
50 g/1¾ oz Gorgonzola cheese, crumbled
25 g/1 oz Parmesan cheese, grated
225 g/8 oz tofu (bean curd), sliced
2 tbsp chopped fresh thyme
salt and pepper
thyme sprigs, to garnish

1 Cook the potato wedges in a saucepan of boiling water for 10 minutes. Drain thoroughly.

2 Meanwhile, melt the butter in a saucepan. Add the sliced onion and garlic and fry gently for 2–3 minutes.

3 Stir the flour into the pan and cook for 1 minute. Gradually add the milk and bring to the boil, stirring constantly.

4 Reduce the heat and add the artichoke hearts, mixed vegetables, half of each of the 4 cheeses and the tofu (bean curd) to the pan, mixing well. Stir in the chopped fresh thyme and season with salt and pepper to taste.

5 Arrange a layer of parboiled potato wedges in the base of a shallow ovenproof dish. Spoon the vegetable mixture over the top and cover with the remaining potato wedges. Sprinkle the rest of the 4 cheeses over the top.

6 Cook in a preheated oven, 200°C/400°F/ Gas Mark 6, for 30 minutes or until the potatoes are cooked and the top is golden brown. Serve the bake garnished with fresh thyme sprigs.

Potato & Aubergine (Eggplant) Gratin

Serves 4

INGREDIENTS

450 g/1/lb waxy potatoes, sliced
1 tbsp vegetable oil
1 onion, chopped
2 garlic cloves, crushed
450 g/1 lb tofu (bean curd), diced
2 tbsp tomato purée (paste)
2 tbsp plain (all-purpose) flour
300 ml/½ pint/1¼ cups vegetable stock
2 large tomatoes, sliced
1 aubergine (eggplant), sliced
2 tbsp chopped fresh thyme
450 g/1/lb natural yogurt
2 eggs, beaten
salt and pepper

1 Cook the sliced potatoes in a saucepan of boiling water for 10 minutes until tender but not breaking up. Drain and set aside.

2 Heat the oil in a pan and fry the onion and garlic for 2–3 minutes.

3 Add the diced tofu (bean curd), tomato purée (paste) and flour and cook for 1 minute. Gradually stir in the vegetable stock and bring to the boil, stirring constantly. Reduce the heat and leave to simmer for 10 minutes.

4 Arrange a layer of the potato slices in the base of a deep ovenproof dish. Spoon the tofu (bean curd) mixture on top.

5 Layer the tomatoes, then the aubergine (eggplant) and then the remaining potato slices on top of the tofu mixture, making sure that it is completely covered.

6 Mix the yogurt and beaten eggs together in a bowl and season well with salt and pepper. Spoon the yogurt topping over the sliced potatoes.

7 Cook in a preheated oven, 190°C/375°F/ Gas Mark 5, for 35–45 minutes or until the topping is browned. Serve hot, with a crisp green salad.

VARIATION

You can use marinated or smoked tofu (bean curd) for extra flavour, if you wish.

Spicy Potato & Nut Terrine

Serves 4

INGREDIENTS

225 g/8 oz floury (mealy) potatoes, diced
225 g/8 oz pecan nuts
225 g/8 oz unsalted cashew nuts
1 onion, chopped finely
2 garlic cloves, crushed
125 g/4½ oz open cap mushrooms, diced
25 g/1 oz/2 tbsp butter
2 tbsp chopped mixed herbs
1 tsp paprika
1 tsp ground cumin
1 tsp ground coriander
4 eggs, beaten
125 g/4½ oz full fat soft cheese
50 g/2 oz Parmesan cheese, grated
salt and pepper

SAUCE:
3 large tomatoes, peeled, seeded and chopped
2 tbsp tomato purée (paste)
85 ml/3 fl oz/⅓ cup red wine
1 tbsp red wine vinegar
pinch of caster sugar

1 Lightly grease a 1.1 kg/2 lb loaf tin (pan) and line with baking parchment.

2 Cook the potatoes in a pan of boiling water for 10 minutes or until cooked through. Drain and mash the potatoes.

3 Finely chop the pecan and cashew nuts or work in a food processor. Mix the nuts with the onion, garlic and mushrooms. Melt the butter in a frying pan (skillet) and cook the nut mixture for 5–7 minutes. Add the herbs and spices to the pan. Stir in the eggs, cheeses, potatoes and season.

4 Spoon the mixture into the prepared loaf tin (pan), pressing down firmly. Cook in a preheated oven, 190°C/375°F/Gas Mark 5, for 1 hour or until set.

5 To make the sauce, mix the tomatoes, tomato purée (paste), wine, wine vinegar and sugar in a pan and bring to the boil, stirring. Cook for 10 minutes or until the tomatoes have reduced. Pass the sauce through a sieve or blend in a food processor for 30 seconds. Turn the terrine out of the tin (pan) and cut into slices. Serve with a little of the tomato sauce.

Pies & Bakes

The following chapter includes a range of hearty savoury pies and bakes which are ideal for cold autumn (fall) and winter evenings. However, a few less robust meals are also included which are more suitable for a light spring or summer meal. Many of the recipes are adaptable and you may like to substitute your favourite vegetables for the ones suggested in the recipe, or vary them according to seasonal availability.

There are both sweet and savoury recipes in this chapter, as the sweet potato lends itself to sweeter dishes, mixed with fruit and spices. Also included are a few bread recipes, as the potato makes excellent bread; an assortment of fabulous pies using different pastries; and pastry bites, such as pasties. This chapter contains something for every occasion, illustrating how well the potato lends itself to a wide variety of dishes.

Potato, Beef & Leek Pasties

Makes 4

INGREDIENTS

225 g/8 oz waxy potatoes, diced
1 small carrot, diced
225 g/8 oz beef steak, cubed
1 leek, sliced
225 g/8 oz ready made shortcrust pastry (pie dough)
15 g/$^{1}/_{2}$ oz/1 tbsp butter
salt and pepper
1 egg, beaten

1 Lightly grease a baking (cookie) sheet.

2 Mix the potatoes, carrots, beef and leek in a large bowl. Season well with salt and pepper.

3 Divide the pastry (pie dough) into 4 equal portions. On a lightly floured surface, roll each portion into a 20 cm/8 inch round.

4 Spoon the potato mixture on to one half of each round, to within 1 cm/$^{1}/_{2}$ inch of the edge. Top the potato mixture with the butter, dividing it equally between the rounds. Brush the pastry (pie dough) edge with a little of the beaten egg.

5 Fold the pastry (pie dough) over to encase the filling and crimp the edges together.

6 Transfer the pasties to the prepared baking (cookie) sheet and brush them with the beaten egg.

7 Cook in a preheated oven, 200°C/400°F/ Gas Mark 6, for 20 minutes. Reduce the oven temperature to 160°C/325°F/Gas Mark 3 and cook the pasties for a further 30 minutes until cooked.

8 Serve the pasties with a crisp salad or onion gravy.

COOK'S TIP

These pasties can be made in advance and frozen.

VARIATION

Use other types of meat, such as pork or chicken, in the pasties and add chunks of apple in step 2, if preferred.

Potato & Tomato Calzone

Makes 4

INGREDIENTS

DOUGH:
450 g/1 lb/4 cups white bread flour
1 tsp easy blend dried yeast
300 ml/½ pint/1¼ cups vegetable stock
1 tbsp clear honey
1 tsp caraway seeds
milk, for glazing

FILLING:
225 g/8 oz waxy potatoes, diced
1 tbsp vegetable oil
1 onion, halved and sliced
2 garlic cloves, crushed
40 g/1½ oz sun-dried tomatoes
2 tbsp chopped fresh basil
2 tbsp tomato purée (paste)
2 celery sticks, sliced
50 g/2 oz Mozzarella cheese, grated

1 To make the dough, sift the flour into a large mixing bowl and stir in the yeast. Make a well in the centre of the mixture.

2 Stir in the vegetable stock, honey and caraway seeds and bring the mixture together to form a dough.

3 Turn the dough out on to a lightly floured surface and knead for 8 minutes until smooth. Place the dough in a lightly oiled mixing bowl, cover and leave to rise in a warm place for 1 hour or until it has doubled in size.

4 Meanwhile, make the filling. Heat the oil in a frying pan (skillet) and add all the remaining ingredients except for the cheese. Cook for about 5 minutes, stirring.

5 Divide the risen dough into 4 pieces. On a lightly floured surface, roll them out to form four 18 cm/7 inch circles. Spoon equal amounts of the filling on to one half of each circle.

6 Sprinkle the cheese over the filling. Brush the edge of the dough with milk and fold the dough over to form 4 semi-circles, pressing to seal the edges.

7 Place on a non-stick baking (cookie) sheet and brush with milk. Cook in a preheated oven, 220°C/425°F/Gas Mark 7, for 30 minutes until golden and risen.

Potato & Meat Filo Parcels

Serves 4

INGREDIENTS

225 g/8 oz waxy potatoes, diced finely
1 tbsp vegetable oil
125 g/4½ oz ground beef
1 leek, sliced
1 small yellow (bell) pepper, diced finely
125 g/4½ oz button mushrooms, sliced
1 tbsp plain (all-purpose) flour
1 tbsp tomato purée (paste)
85 ml/3 fl oz/⅓ cup red wine
85 ml/3 fl oz/⅓ cup beef stock
1 tbsp chopped fresh rosemary
225 g/8 oz filo pastry (pie dough), thawed if frozen
2 tbsp butter, melted
salt and pepper

1 Cook the diced potatoes in a saucepan of boiling water for 5 minutes. Drain and set aside.

2 Meanwhile, heat the oil in a saucepan and fry the ground beef, leek, yellow (bell) pepper and mushrooms over a low heat for 5 minutes.

3 Stir in the flour and tomato purée (paste) and cook for 1 minute. Gradually add the red wine and beef stock, stirring to thicken. Add the rosemary, season to taste with salt and pepper and leave to cool slightly.

4 Lay 4 sheets of filo pastry (pie dough) on a work surface (counter) or board. Brush each sheet with butter and lay a second layer of filo on top. Trim the sheets to make four 20 cm/8 inch squares.

5 Brush the edges of the pastry with a little butter. Spoon a quarter of the beef mixture into the centre of each square. Bring up the corners and the sides of the squares to form a parcel, scrunching the edges together. Make sure that the parcels are well sealed by pressing the pastry (pie dough) together, otherwise the filling will leak.

6 Place the parcels on a baking (cookie) sheet and brush with butter. Bake in a preheated oven, 180°C/350°F/Gas Mark 4, for 20 minutes. Serve hot.

4

5

5

Carrot-Topped Beef Pie

Serves 4

INGREDIENTS

450 g/1 lb ground beef
1 onion, chopped
1 garlic clove, crushed
1 tbsp plain (all-purpose) flour
300 ml/½ pint/1¼ cups beef stock
2 tbsp tomato purée (paste)
1 celery stick, chopped
3 tbsp chopped fresh parsley
1 tbsp Worcestershire sauce
675 g/1½ lb floury (mealy) potatoes, diced
2 large carrots, diced
25 g/1 oz/2 tbsp butter
3 tbsp milk
salt and pepper

1 Dry fry the beef in a large pan set over a high heat for 3–4 minutes or until sealed. Add the onion and garlic and cook for a further 5 minutes, stirring.

2 Add the flour and cook for 1 minute. Gradually blend in the beef stock and tomato purée (paste). Stir in the celery, 1 tbsp of the parsley and the Worcestershire sauce. Season to taste with salt and pepper.

3 Bring the mixture to the boil, then reduce the heat and simmer for 20–25 minutes. Spoon the beef mixture into a 1.1 litre/2 pint/5 cup pie dish.

4 Meanwhile, cook the potatoes and carrots in a saucepan of boiling water for 10 minutes. Drain and mash them together.

5 Stir the butter, milk and the remaining parsley into the potato and carrot mixture and season. Spoon the potato on top of the beef mixture to cover it completely; alternatively, pipe the potato with a piping (pastry) bag.

6 Cook the pie in a preheated oven, 190°C/375°F/Gas Mark 5, for 45 minutes or until cooked through. Serve hot.

VARIATION

You can use ground lamb, turkey or pork instead of the beef, adding appropriate herbs, such as rosemary and sage, for added flavour.

Potato, Beef & Kidney Pie

Serves 4

INGREDIENTS

225 g/8 oz waxy potatoes, cubed
25 g/1 oz/2 tbsp butter
450 g/1 lb lean steak, cubed
150 g/5½ oz ox kidney, cored and chopped
12 shallots
25 g/1 oz/¼ cup plain (all-purpose) flour
150 ml/¼ pint/⅔ cup beef stock
150 ml/¼ pint/⅔ cup stout
225 g/8 oz ready-made puff pastry (pie dough)
1 egg, beaten
salt and pepper

1 Cook the cubed potatoes in a saucepan of boiling water for 10 minutes. Drain thoroughly.

2 Meanwhile, melt the butter in a saucepan and add the steak cubes and the kidney. Cook for 5 minutes, stirring until the meat is sealed on all sides.

3 Add the shallots and cook for a further 3–4 minutes. Stir in the flour and cook for 1 minute. Gradually stir in the beef stock and stout and bring to the boil, stirring constantly.

4 Stir the potatoes into the meat mixture and season with salt and pepper. Reduce the heat until the mixture is simmering. Cover the saucepan and cook for 1 hour, stirring occasionally.

5 Spoon the beef mixture into the base of a pie dish. Roll the pastry (pie dough) on a lightly floured surface until 1 cm/½ inch larger than the top of the dish.

6 Cut a strip of pastry (pie dough) long enough and wide enough to fit around the edge of the dish. Brush the edge of the dish with beaten egg and press the pastry (pie dough) strip around the edge. Brush with egg and place the pastry (pie dough) lid on top. Crimp to seal the edge and brush with beaten egg.

7 Cook in a preheated oven, 230°C/450°F/Gas Mark 8, for 20–25 minutes or until the pastry has risen and is golden. Serve hot, straight from the dish.

Raised Potato, Pork & Apple Pie

Serves 8

INGREDIENTS

FILLING:
900 g/2 lb waxy potatoes, sliced
25 g/1 oz/2 tbsp butter
2 tbsp vegetable oil
450 g/1 lb lean pork, cubed
2 onions, sliced
4 garlic cloves, crushed
4 tbsp tomato purée (paste)
600 ml/1 pint/2½ cups stock
2 tbsp chopped fresh sage
2 dessert apples, peeled and sliced
salt and pepper

PASTRY (PIE DOUGH):
675 g/1½ lb/6 cups plain (all-purpose) flour
pinch of salt
50 g/1¾ oz/10 tsp butter
125 g/4½ oz/½ cup lard (shortening)
300 ml/½ pint/1¼ cups water
1 egg, beaten
1 tsp gelatine

1 Cook the potatoes in boiling water for 10 minutes. Drain and set aside. Heat the butter and oil in a flameproof casserole dish and fry the pork until browned, turning. Add the onion and garlic and cook for 5 minutes. Stir in the rest of the filling ingredients, except for the potatoes and the apples. Reduce the heat, cover and simmer for 1½ hours. Drain the stock from the casserole dish and reserve. Leave the pork to cool.

2 To make the pastry (pie dough), sieve the flour into a bowl. Add the salt and make a well in the centre. Melt the butter and lard in a pan with the water; then bring to the boil. Pour into the flour and mix to form a dough. Turn on to a floured surface and knead until smooth. Reserve a quarter of the dough and use the rest to line the base and sides of a large pie tin (pan) or deep 20 cm/8 inch loose-bottom cake tin (pan).

3 Layer the pork, potatoes and the apple in the base. Roll out the reserved pastry (pie dough) to make a lid. Dampen the edges and place the lid on top, sealing well. Brush with egg and make a hole in the top. Cook in a preheated oven, 200°C/400°F/Gas Mark 6, for 30 minutes, then at 160°C/325°F/Gas Mark 3 for 45 minutes. Dissolve the gelatine in the reserved stock and pour into the hole in the lid as the pie cools. Serve well chilled.

Potato, Sausage & Onion Pie

Serves 4

INGREDIENTS

2 large waxy potatoes, unpeeled and sliced
25 g/1 oz/2 tbsp butter
4 thick pork and herb sausages
1 leek, sliced
2 garlic cloves, crushed
150 ml/¼ pint/⅔ cup vegetable stock
150 ml/¼ pint/⅔ cup dry cider or apple juice
2 tbsp chopped fresh sage
2 tbsp cornflour (cornstarch)
4 tbsp water
75 g/2¾ oz mature (sharp) cheese, grated
salt and pepper

1 Cook the sliced potatoes in a saucepan of boiling water for 10 minutes. Drain and set aside.

2 Meanwhile, melt the butter in a frying pan (skillet) and cook the sausages for 8–10 minutes, turning them frequently so that they brown on all sides. Remove the sausages from the pan (skillet) and cut them into thick slices.

3 Add the leek, garlic and sausage slices to the pan (skillet) and cook for 2–3 minutes.

4 Add the vegetable stock, cider or apple juice and chopped sage. Season with salt and pepper. Blend the cornflour (cornstarch) with the water. Stir it into the pan (skillet) and bring to the boil, stirring until the sauce is thick and clear. Spoon the mixture into the base of a deep pie dish.

5 Layer the potato slices on top of the sausage mixture to cover it completely. Season with salt and pepper and sprinkle the grated cheese over the top.

6 Cook in a preheated oven, 190°C/375°F/ Gas Mark 5, for 25–30 minutes or until the potatoes are cooked and the cheese is golden brown. Serve the pie hot.

VARIATION

Other vegetables, such as broccoli or cauliflower, can be added to the filling. You can use white wine instead of the cider or apple juice, if you prefer.

Potato & Broccoli Pie

Serves 4

INGREDIENTS

450 g/1 lb waxy potatoes, cut into chunks
25 g/1 oz/2 tbsp butter
1 tbsp vegetable oil
175 g/6 oz lean pork, cubed
1 red onion, cut into 8
25 g/1 oz plain (all-purpose) flour
150 ml/$^1/_4$ pint/$^2/_3$ cup vegetable stock
150 ml/$^1/_4$ pint/$^2/_3$ cup milk
75 g/2$^3/_4$ oz dolcelatte, crumbled
175 g/6 oz broccoli florets
25 g/1 oz walnuts
225 g/8 oz ready-made puff pastry (pie dough)
milk, for glazing
salt and pepper

1 Cook the potato chunks in a saucepan of boiling water for 5 minutes. Drain and set aside.

2 Meanwhile, heat the butter and oil in a heavy-based pan. Add the pork cubes and cook for 5 minutes, turning until browned.

3 Add the onion and cook for a further 2 minutes. Stir in the flour and cook for 1 minute, then gradually stir in the vegetable stock and milk. Bring to the boil, stirring constantly.

4 Add the cheese, broccoli, potatoes and walnuts to the pan and simmer for 5 minutes. Season with salt and pepper, then spoon the mixture into a pie dish.

5 On a floured surface, roll out the pastry (pie dough) until 2.5 cm/1 inch larger than the dish. Cut a 2.5 cm/1 inch wide strip from the pastry (pie dough). Dampen the edge of the dish and place the pastry (pie dough) strip around it. Brush with milk and put the pastry (pie dough) lid on top.

6 Seal and crimp the edges and make 2 small slits in the centre of the lid. Brush with milk and cook in a preheated oven, 200°C/400°F/Gas Mark 6, for 25 minutes or until the pastry has risen and is golden.

COOK'S TIP

Use a hard cheese such as mature (sharp) cheese instead of the dolcelatte, if you prefer.

Potato & Ham Pie

Serves 4

INGREDIENTS

225 g/8 oz waxy potatoes, cubed
25 g/1 oz/2 tbsp butter
8 shallots, halved
225 g/8 oz smoked ham, cubed
25 g/1 oz/¼ cup plain (all-purpose) flour
300 ml/½ pint/1¼ cups milk
2 tbsp wholegrain mustard
50 g/1¾ oz pineapple, cubed

PASTRY (PIE DOUGH):
225 g/8 oz/2 cups plain (all-purpose) flour
½ tsp dry mustard
pinch of salt
pinch of cayenne pepper
150 g/5½ oz/⅔ cup butter
125 g/4½ oz mature (sharp) cheese, grated
2 egg yolks, plus extra for brushing
4–6 tsp cold water

1 Cook the potato cubes in a saucepan of boiling water for 10 minutes. Drain and set aside.

2 Meanwhile, melt the butter in a saucepan, add the shallots and fry gently for 3–4 minutes until they begin to colour.

3 Add the ham and cook for 2–3 minutes. Stir in the flour and cook for 1 minute. Gradually stir in the milk. Add the mustard and pineapple and bring to the boil, stirring. Season well with salt and pepper and add the potatoes.

4 Sieve the flour for the pastry (pie dough) into a bowl with the mustard, salt and cayenne. Rub the butter into the mixture until it resembles breadcrumbs. Add the cheese and mix to form a dough with the egg yolks and water.

5 On a floured surface, roll out half of the pastry and line a shallow pie dish; trim the edges.

6 Spoon the filling into the pie dish. Brush the edges of the pastry (pie dough) with water.

7 Roll out the remaining pastry (pie dough) to make a lid and press it on top of the pie, sealing the edges. Decorate the top of the pie with the pastry (pie dough) trimmings. Brush the pie with egg yolk and cook in a preheated oven, 190°C/375°F/Gas Mark 5, for 40–45 minutes or until the pastry is cooked and golden.

3

3

5

Potato & Turkey Pie

Serves 4

INGREDIENTS

300 g/10½ oz waxy potatoes, diced
25 g/1 oz/2 tbsp butter
1 tbsp vegetable oil
300 g/10½ oz lean turkey meat, cubed
1 red onion, halved and sliced
25 g/1 oz/¼ cup plain (all-purpose) flour
300 ml/½ pint/1¼ cups milk
150 ml/¼ pint/⅔ cup double (heavy) cream
2 celery sticks, sliced
75 g/2¾ oz dried apricots, chopped
25 g/1 oz walnut pieces
2 tbsp chopped fresh parsley
salt and pepper
225 g/8 oz ready made shortcrust pastry (pie dough)
beaten egg, for brushing

1 Cook the diced potatoes in a saucepan of boiling water for 10 minutes until tender. Drain and set aside.

2 Meanwhile, heat the butter and oil in a saucepan. Add the turkey and cook for 5 minutes, turning until browned.

3 Add the sliced onion and cook for 2–3 minutes. Stir in the flour and cook for 1 minute. Gradually stir in the milk and the double (heavy) cream. Bring to the boil, stirring, then reduce the heat until the mixture is simmering.

4 Stir in the celery, apricots, walnut pieces, parsley and potatoes. Season well with salt and pepper. Spoon the potato and turkey mixture into the base of a 1.1 litre/2 pint/5 cup pie dish.

5 On a lightly floured surface, roll out the pastry (pie dough) until it is 2.5 cm/1 inch larger than the dish. Trim a 2.5 cm/1 inch wide strip from the pastry (pie dough) and place the strip on the dampened rim of the dish. Brush with water and cover with the pastry (pie dough) lid, pressing to seal the edges.

6 Brush the top of the pie with beaten egg and cook in a preheated oven, 200°C/400°F/Gas Mark 6, for 25–30 minutes or until the pastry is cooked and golden brown. Serve at once.

2

3

4

Potato Crisp Pie

Serves 4

INGREDIENTS

2 large waxy potatoes, sliced
60 g/2 oz/¼ cup butter
1 skinned chicken breast fillet, about 175 g/6 oz
2 garlic cloves, crushed
4 spring onions (scallions), sliced
25 g/1 oz/¼ cup plain (all-purpose) flour
150 ml/¼ pint/⅔ cup dry white wine
150 ml/¼ pint/⅔ cup double (heavy) cream
225 g/8 oz broccoli florets
4 large tomatoes, sliced
75 g/3 oz Gruyère cheese, sliced
225 ml/8 fl oz/1 cup natural yogurt
25 g/1 oz/⅓ cup rolled oats, toasted

1 Cook the potatoes in a saucepan of boiling water for 10 minutes. Drain and set aside.

2 Meanwhile, melt the butter in a frying pan (skillet). Cut the chicken into strips and cook for 5 minutes, turning. Add the garlic and spring onions (scallions) and cook for a further 2 minutes.

3 Stir in the flour and cook for 1 minute. Gradually add the wine and cream. Bring to the boil, stirring, then reduce the heat until the sauce is simmering, then cook for 5 minutes.

4 Meanwhile, blanch the broccoli in boiling water, drain and refresh in cold water.

5 Place half of the potatoes in the base of a pie dish and top with half of the tomatoes and half of the broccoli.

6 Spoon the chicken sauce on top and repeat the layers in the same order once more.

7 Arrange the Gruyère cheese on top and spoon over the yogurt. Sprinkle with the oats and cook in a preheated oven, 200°C/400°F/Gas Mark 6, for 25 minutes until the top is golden brown. Serve the pie immediately.

COOK'S TIP

Add chopped nuts, such as pine kernels (nuts), to the topping for extra crunch, if you prefer.

Potato, Leek & Chicken Pie

Serves 4

INGREDIENTS

225 g/8 oz waxy potatoes, cubed
60 g/2 oz/¼ cup butter
1 skinned chicken breast fillet, about 175 g/6 oz, cubed
150 g/5½ oz chestnut mushrooms, sliced
1 leek, sliced
25 g/1 oz/¼ cup plain (all purpose) flour
300 ml/½ pint/1¼ cups milk
1 tbsp Dijon mustard
2 tbsp chopped fresh sage
225 g/8 oz filo pastry (pie dough), thawed if frozen
40 g/1½ oz/3 tbsp butter, melted
salt and pepper

1 Cook the potato cubes in a saucepan of boiling water for 5 minutes. Drain and set aside.

2 Melt the butter in a frying pan (skillet) and cook the chicken cubes for 5 minutes or until browned all over.

3 Add the leek and mushrooms and cook for 3 minutes, stirring. Stir in the flour and cook for 1 minute. Gradually add the milk and bring to the boil. Add the mustard, chopped sage and potato cubes, then leave the mixture to simmer for 10 minutes.

4 Meanwhile, line a deep pie dish with half of the sheets of filo pastry (pie dough). Spoon the sauce into the dish and cover with one sheet of pastry (pie dough). Brush the pastry (pie dough) with butter and lay another sheet on top. Brush this sheet with butter.

5 Cut the remaining filo pastry (pie dough) into strips and fold them on to the top of the pie to create a ruffled effect. Brush the strips with the melted butter and cook in a preheated oven 180°C/350°F/Gas Mark 4 for 45 minutes or until golden brown and crisp. Serve hot.

COOK'S TIP

If the top of the pie starts to brown too quickly, cover it with foil halfway through the cooking time, to allow the pastry base to cook through without the top burning.

3

4

5

Layered Fish & Potato Pie

Serves 4

INGREDIENTS

900 g/2 lb waxy potatoes, sliced
60 g/2 oz/$^1/_4$ cup butter
1 red onion, halved and sliced
50 g/1$^3/_4$ oz/$^1/_3$ cup plain (all-purpose) flour
450 ml/$^3/_4$ pint/2 cups milk
150 ml/$^1/_4$ pint double (heavy) cream
225 g/8 oz smoked haddock fillet, cubed
225 g/8 oz cod fillet, cubed
1 red (bell) pepper, diced
125 g/4$^1/_2$ oz broccoli florets
50 g/1$^3/_4$ oz Parmesan cheese, grated
salt and pepper

1 Cook the sliced potatoes in a saucepan of boiling water for 10 minutes. Drain and set aside.

2 Meanwhile, melt the butter in a saucepan, add the onion and fry gently for 3–4 minutes.

3 Add the flour and cook for 1 minute. Blend in the milk and cream and bring to the boil, stirring until the sauce has thickened.

4 Arrange half of the potato slices in the base of a shallow ovenproof dish.

5 Add the fish, diced (bell) pepper and broccoli to the sauce and cook over a low heat for 10 minutes. Season with salt and pepper, then spoon the mixture over the potatoes in the dish.

6 Arrange the remaining potato slices in a layer over the fish mixture. Sprinkle the Parmesan cheese over the top.

7 Cook in a preheated oven, 180°C/350°F Gas Mark 4, for 30 minutes or until the potatoes are cooked and the top is golden.

COOK'S TIP

Choose your favourite combination of fish, adding salmon or various shellfish for special occasions.

Potato-Topped Smoked Fish Pie

Serves 4

INGREDIENTS

450 g/1 lb floury (mealy) potatoes, diced
225 g/8 oz swede, diced
60 g/2 oz/$^1/_4$ cup butter
1 leek, sliced
50 g/1$^3/_4$ oz baby sweetcorn cobs, sliced
1 courgette (zucchini), halved and sliced
50 g/1$^3/_4$ oz/$^1/_3$ cup plain (all-purpose) flour
300 ml/$^1/_2$ pint/1$^1/_4$ cups milk
150 ml/$^1/_4$ pint/$^2/_3$ cup fish stock
150 ml/$^1/_4$ pint/$^2/_3$ cup double (heavy) cream
450 g/1 lb smoked cod fillet, cut into cubes
few drops of Tabasco sauce
125 g/4$^1/_2$ oz cooked peeled prawns (shrimp)
2 tbsp chopped fresh parsley
2 tbsp grated Parmesan cheese
salt and pepper

1 Cook the potatoes and swede in a saucepan of boiling water for 20 minutes until very tender. Drain and mash until smooth.

2 Meanwhile, melt the butter in a saucepan, add the leeks, sweetcorn cobs and courgette (zucchini) and fry gently for 3–4 minutes, stirring.

3 Add the flour and cook for 1 minute. Gradually blend in the milk, fish stock and cream and bring to the boil, stirring until the mixture begins to thicken.

4 Stir in the fish, reduce the heat and cook for 5 minutes. Add the Tabasco sauce, prawns (shrimp), half of the parsley and season. Spoon the mixture into the base of an ovenproof dish.

5 Mix the remaining parsley into the potato and swede mixture, season and spoon or pipe on to the fish mixture, covering it completely. Sprinkle with the grated cheese and cook in a preheated oven, 180°C/350°F/Gas Mark 4, for 20 minutes. Serve the pie immediately.

VARIATION

Add cooked mashed parsnip to the potato instead of the swede.

2

3

4

Potato, Tuna & Cheese Quiche

Serves 4

INGREDIENTS

450 g/1 lb floury (mealy) potatoes, diced
25 g/1 oz/2 tbsp butter
6 tbsp plain (all-purpose) flour

FILLING:
1 tbsp vegetable oil
1 shallot, chopped
1 garlic clove, crushed
1 red (bell) pepper, diced
175g/6 oz can tuna in brine, drained
50 g/1¾ oz canned sweetcorn, drained
150 ml/¼ pint/⅔ cup milk
3 eggs, beaten
1 tbsp chopped fresh dill
50 g/1¾ oz mature (sharp) cheese, grated
salt and pepper

TO GARNISH:
fresh dill sprigs
lemon wedges

1 Cook the potatoes in a pan of boiling water for 10 minutes or until tender. Drain and mash the potatoes. Add the butter and flour and mix to form a dough.

2 Knead the potato dough on a floured surface and press the mixture into a 20 cm/8 in flan tin (pan). Prick the base with a fork. Line with baking parchment and baking beans and bake blind in a preheated oven, 200°C/400°F/Gas Mark 6, for 20 minutes.

3 Heat the oil in a frying pan (skillet), add the onion, garlic and (bell) pepper and fry gently for 5 minutes. Drain well and spoon into the flan case (shell). Flake the tuna and arrange it over the top.

4 In a bowl, mix the milk, eggs and chopped dill together. Season with salt and pepper.

5 Pour the egg and dill mixture into the flan case (shell) and sprinkle the grated cheese on top.

6 Bake in the oven for 20 minutes or until the filling has set. Garnish the quiche with fresh dill and lemon wedges. Serve with mixed vegetables or salad.

VARIATION

Use any other cooked fish of your choice, or canned crab meat instead of the tuna, if you prefer.

Potato-Topped Lentil Bake

Serves 4

INGREDIENTS

TOPPING:
675 g/1½ lb floury (mealy) potatoes, diced
25 g/1 oz/2 tbsp butter
1 tbsp milk
50 g/1¾ oz chopped pecan nuts
2 tbsp chopped fresh thyme
thyme sprigs, to garnish

FILLING:
225 g/8 oz/1 cup red lentils
60 g/2 oz/¼ cup butter
1 leek, sliced
2 garlic cloves, crushed
1 celery stick, chopped
125 g/4½ oz broccoli florets
175 g/6 oz smoked tofu (bean curd), cubed
2 tsp tomato purée (paste)
salt and pepper

1 To make the topping, cook the potatoes in a saucepan of boiling water for 10–15 minutes or until cooked through. Drain well, add the butter and milk and mash thoroughly. Stir in the pecan nuts and chopped thyme and set aside.

2 Cook the lentils in boiling water for 20–30 minutes or until tender. Drain and set aside.

3 Melt the butter in a pan, add the leek, garlic, celery and broccoli. Cook for 5 minutes, then add the tofu (bean curd) cubes.

4 Stir the lentils into the tofu (bean curd) and vegetable mixture with the tomato purée (paste). Season with salt and pepper to taste, then turn the mixture into the base of a shallow ovenproof dish.

5 Spoon the mashed potato on top of the lentil mixture to cover it completely.

6 Cook in a preheated oven, 200°C/400°F/Gas Mark 6, for 30–35 minutes or until the topping is golden. Garnish with sprigs of fresh thyme and serve hot.

VARIATION

You can use any combination of vegetables in this dish. You can also add sliced cooked meat instead of the cubed tofu (bean curd) for a non-vegetarian dish.

Potato & Aubergine (Eggplant) Layer

Serves 4

INGREDIENTS

3 large waxy potatoes, sliced thinly
1 small aubergine (eggplant), sliced thinly
1 courgette (zucchini), sliced
2 tbsp vegetable oil
1 onion, diced
1 green (bell) pepper, diced
1 tsp cumin seeds
200 g/7 oz can chopped tomatoes
2 tbsp chopped fresh basil
175 g/6 oz Mozarella cheese, sliced
225 g/8 oz tofu (bean curd), sliced
60 g/2 oz/1 cup fresh white breadcrumbs
2 tbsp grated Parmesan cheese
salt and pepper
fresh basil leaves, to garnish

1 Cook the sliced potatoes in a saucepan of boiling water for 5 minutes. Drain and set aside.

2 Lay the aubergine (eggplant) slices on a plate, sprinkle with salt and leave for 20 minutes. Blanch the courgette (zucchini) in boiling water for 2–3 minutes. Drain and set aside.

3 Meanwhile, heat 2 tbsp of the oil in a frying pan (skillet), add the onion and fry gently for 2–3 minutes until softened. Add the (bell) pepper, cumin seeds, basil and canned tomatoes. Season with salt and pepper. Leave the sauce to simmer for 30 minutes.

4 Rinse the aubergine (eggplant) slices and pat dry. Heat the remaining oil in a large frying pan (skillet) and fry the aubergine (eggplant) slices for 3–5 minutes, turning to brown both sides. Drain and set aside.

5 Arrange half of the potato slices in the base of 4 small loose-bottomed flan tins (pans). Cover with half of the courgette (zucchini) slices, half of the aubergine (eggplant) slices and half of the Mozzarella slices. Lay the tofu (bean curd) on top and spoon over the tomato sauce. Repeat the layers of vegetables and cheese.

6 Mix the breadcrumbs and Parmesan together and sprinkle over the top. Cook in a preheated oven, 190°C/375°F/Gas Mark 5, for 25–30 minutes or until golden. Garnish with basil leaves.

Sweet Potato Bread

Makes 1 loaf

INGREDIENTS

225 g/8 oz sweet potatoes, diced
150 ml/¼ pint/⅔ cup tepid water
2 tbsp clear honey
2 tbsp vegetable oil
3 tbsp orange juice
75 g/2⅔ oz/generous ⅓ cup semolina
225 g/8 oz/2 cups white bread flour
7 g sachet easy blend dried yeast
1 tsp ground cinnamon
grated rind of 1 orange
60 g/2 oz/1 cup butter

1 Lightly grease a 675 g/ 11/2 lb loaf tin (pan).

2 Cook the sweet potatoes in a saucepan of boiling water for 10 minutes or until soft. Drain well and mash until smooth.

3 Meanwhile, mix the water, honey, oil, and orange juice together in a large mixing bowl.

4 Add the mashed sweet potatoes, semolina, three quarters of the flour, the yeast, cinnamon and orange rind and mix well to form a dough. Leave to stand for about 10 minutes.

5 Cut the butter into small pieces and knead it into the dough with the remaining flour. Knead for about 5 minutes until the dough is smooth.

6 Place the dough in the prepared loaf tin (pan). Cover and leave in a warm place to rise for 1 hour or until doubled in size.

7 Cook the loaf in a preheated oven, 190°C/ 375°F/Gas Mark 5, for 45–60 minutes or until the base sounds hollow when tapped. Serve the bread warm, cut into slices.

COOK'S TIP

If the baked loaf does not sound hollow on the base when it is tapped, remove it from the tin (pan) and return it to the ovenfor a few extra minutes until thoroughly cooked.

3

4

5

Cheese & Potato Plait

Makes one 450 g/1 lb loaf

INGREDIENTS

175 g/6 oz floury (mealy) potatoes, diced
2 x 7 g sachets easy blend dried yeast
675 g/$1\frac{1}{2}$ lb/6 cups white bread flour
450 ml/$\frac{3}{4}$ pint/2 cups vegetable stock
2 garlic cloves, crushed
2 tbsp chopped fresh rosemary
125 g/$4\frac{1}{2}$ oz Gruyère cheese, grated
1 tbsp vegetable oil
1 tbsp salt

1 Lightly grease and flour a baking (cookie) sheet.

2 Cook the potatoes in a pan of boiling water for 10 minutes or until soft. Drain and mash.

3 Transfer the mashed potatoes to a large mixing bowl, stir in the yeast, flour and stock and mix to form a smooth dough.

4 Add the garlic, rosemary and 75 g/$2\frac{3}{4}$ oz of the cheese and knead the dough for 5 minutes. Make a hollow in the dough, pour in the oil and knead the dough.

5 Cover the dough and leave it to rise in a warm place for $1\frac{1}{2}$ hours or until doubled in size.

6 Knead the dough again and divide it into 3 equal portions. Roll each portion into a 35 cm/14 inch sausage shape.

7 Pressing one end of each of the sausage shapes together, plait the dough and fold the remaining ends under.

8 Place the plait on the baking (cookie) sheet, cover and leave to rise for 30 minutes.

9 Sprinkle the remaining cheese over the top of the plait and cook in a preheated oven, 190°C/375°F/Gas Mark 5, for 40 minutes or until the base of the loaf sounds hollow when tapped. Serve warm.

VARIATION

Instead of making a plait, use the mixture to make a batch of cheesey rolls which would be ideal to serve with hot soup.

Potato & Nutmeg Scones

Makes 8

INGREDIENTS

225 g/8 oz floury (mealy) potatoes, diced
125 g/4½ oz/1 cup plain (all-purpose) flour
1½ tsp baking powder
½ tsp grated nutmeg
50 g/1¾ oz/⅓ cup sultanas (golden raisins)
1 egg, beaten
50 ml/2 fl oz/¼ cup double (heavy) cream
2 tsp soft light brown sugar

1 Line and grease a baking (cookie) sheet.

2 Cook the diced potatoes in a saucepan of boiling water for 10 minutes or until soft. Drain well and mash the potatoes.

3 Transfer the mashed potatoes to a large mixing bowl and stir in the flour, baking powder and nutmeg.

4 Stir in the sultanas (golden raisins), egg and cream and beat the mixture with a spoon until smooth.

5 Shape the mixture into 8 rounds 2 cm/¾ inch thick and put on the baking (cookie) sheet.

6 Cook in a preheated oven, 200°C/400°F/ Gas Mark 6, for about 15 minutes or until the scones have risen and are golden. Sprinkle the scones with sugar and serve warm and spread with butter.

COOK'S TIP

For extra convenience, make a batch of scones in advance and open-freeze them. Thaw thoroughly and warm in a moderate oven when ready to serve.

VARIATION

This recipe may be used to make one large scone 'cake' instead of the 8 small scones, if you prefer.

3

4

5

Potato Muffins

Serves 12

INGREDIENTS

175 g/6 oz floury (mealy) potatoes, diced
75 g/3 oz/$\frac{3}{4}$ cup self raising flour
2 tbsp soft light brown sugar
1 tsp baking powder
125 g/4$\frac{1}{2}$ oz/$\frac{3}{4}$ cup raisins
4 eggs, separated

1 Lightly grease and flour 12 muffin tins (pans).

2 Cook the diced potatoes in a saucepan of boiling water for 10 minutes or until cooked. Drain well and mash until smooth.

3 Transfer the mashed potatoes to a mixing bowl and add the flour, sugar, baking powder, raisins and egg yolks. Stir well to mix thoroughly.

4 In a clean bowl, whisk the egg whites until standing in peaks. Using a metal spoon, gently fold them into the potato mixture until fully incorporated.

5 Divide the mixture between the prepared tins (pans).

6 Cook in a preheated oven, 200°C/400°F/ Gas Mark 6, for 10 minutes. Reduce the oven temperature to 160°C/ 325°F/Gas Mark 3 and cook the muffins for 7–10 minutes or until risen.

7 Remove the muffins from the tins (pans) and serve warm.

COOK'S TIP

Instead of spreading the muffins with plain butter, serve them with cinnamon butter made by blending 60 g/2 oz/$\frac{1}{2}$ cup butter with a large pinch of ground cinnamon.

VARIATION

Other flavourings, such as cinnamon or nutmeg, can be added to the mixture, if you prefer.

3

4

5

Fruity Potato Cake

Makes one 18 cm/7 inch cake

INGREDIENTS

675 g/1½ lb sweet potatoes, diced
1 tbsp butter, melted
125 g/4½ oz demerara (brown crystal) sugar
3 eggs
3 tbsp milk
1 tbsp lemon juice
grated rind of 1 lemon
1 tsp caraway seeds
125 g/4½ oz dried fruits, such as apple, pear or mango, chopped
2 tsp baking powder

1 Lightly grease an 18 cm/7 inch square cake tin (pan).

2 Cook the sweet potatoes in boiling water for 10 minutes or until soft. Drain and mash the sweet potatoes until smooth.

3 Transfer the mashed sweet potatoes to a mixing bowl whilst still hot and add the butter and sugar, mixing to dissolve.

4 Beat in the eggs, lemon juice and rind, caraway seeds and chopped dried fruit. Add the baking powder and mix well.

5 Pour the mixture into the prepared cake tin (pan).

6 Cook in a preheated oven, 160°C/325°F/ Gas Mark 3, for 1–1¼ hours or until cooked through. Remove the cake from the tin (pan) and transfer to a wire rack to cool. Cut into thick slices to serve.

VARIATION

Add a few drops of rum or brandy to the mixture with the eggs and lemon juice in step 4, if you wish.

COOK'S TIP

This cake is ideal as a special occasion dessert. It can be made in advance and frozen until required. Wrap the cake in cling film (plastic wrap) and freeze. Thaw at room temperature for 24 hours and warm through in a moderate oven before serving.

Index

Index compiled by Hilary Bird.